# Physical Characteristics of the Cocker Spaniel

## (from the American Kennel Club breed standard)

**Body:** The chest is deep, its lowest point no higher than the elbows, its front sufficiently wide...yet not so wide as to interfere with the straightforward movement of the forelegs. Ribs are deep and well sprung. Back is strong and sloping evenly and slightly downward from the shoulders to the set-on of the docked tail. The docked tail is set on and carried on a line with the topline of the back, or slightly higher.

**Hindquarters:** Hips are wide and quarters well rounded and muscular. When viewed from behind, the hind legs are parallel. The hind legs are strongly boned, and muscled with moderate angulation at the stifle and powerful, clearly defined thighs. The stifle is strong. The hocks are strong and well let down.

**Proportion:** The measurement from the breast bone to back of thigh is slightly longer than the measurement from the highest point of withers to the ground.

**Color and Markings:** Black Variety, any Solid Color Other than Black (ASCOB), Parti-Color Variety.

**Size:** The ideal height at the withers for an adult dog is 15 inches and for an adult bitch, 14 inches.

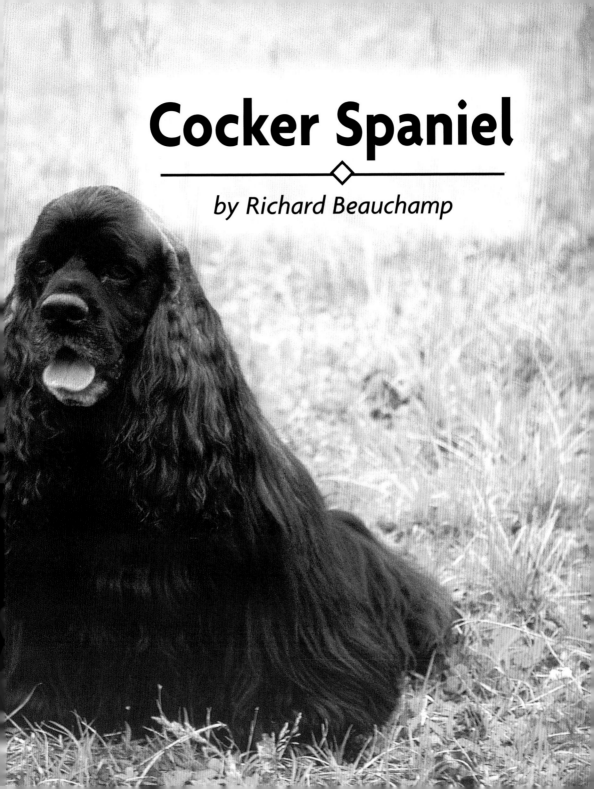

# Cocker Spaniel

by Richard Beauchamp

## 9

## History of the Cocker Spaniel

Trace the ancient beginnings of the Cocker Spaniel as a working gun dog and follow its spread in popularity around the world as a companion dog, show dog, competition dog and ambassador of canine good will.

## 20

## Characteristics of the Cocker Spaniel

Merry, sporting, outgoing and more! Find out about the traits that make the Cocker Spaniel a popular choice for a companion dog. Discussed here are the personality and physical traits of the Cocker as well as breed-specific health concerns.

## 30

## Breed Standard for the Cocker Spaniel

Learn the requirements of a well-bred Cocker Spaniel by studying the description of the breed as set forth in the American Kennel Club's breed standard. Both show dogs and pets must possess key characteristics as outlined in the breed standard.

## 37

## Your Puppy Cocker Spaniel

Be advised about choosing a reputable breeder and selecting a healthy, typical puppy. Understand the responsibilities of ownership, including home preparation, acclimatization, the vet and prevention of common puppy problems.

## 62

## Everyday Care of Your Cocker Spaniel

Enter into a sensible discussion of dietary and feeding considerations, exercise, grooming, traveling and identification of your dog. This chapter discusses Cocker Spaniel care for all stages of development.

## 82

## Training Your Cocker Spaniel

*By Charlotte Schwartz*
Be informed about the importance of training your Cocker Spaniel from the basics of housebreaking and understanding the development of a young dog to executing obedience commands (sit, stay, down, etc.).

# Contents

## Health Care of Your Cocker Spaniel    106

Discover how to select a qualified vet and care for your dog at all stages of life. Topics include vaccinations, skin problems, dealing with external and internal parasites and common medical and behavioral conditions.

## Your Senior Cocker Spaniel    135

Consider the care of your senior Cocker Spaniel, including the proper diet for a senior. Recognize the signs of an aging dog, both behavioral and medical; implement a special-care program with your vet and become comfortable with making the final decisions and arrangements for your senior Cocker Spaniel.

## Showing Your Cocker Spaniel    142

Enter the world of showing dogs. Learn about the American Kennel Club, the different types of shows and the making of a champion. Go beyond the conformation ring to find out about competitive trials and performance events.

Kennel Club Books® Cocker Spaniel
ISBN: 1-59378-233-0

Copyright © 2003, 2006 • Kennel Club Books, LLC
308 Main Street, Allenhurst, NJ 07711 USA
Cover Design Patented: US 6,435,559 B2 • Printed in South Korea

10 9 8 7 6 5 4 3

Photography by:
Norvia Behling, T. J. Calhoun, Carolina Biological Supply, Doskocil, Isabelle Français, James Hayden-Yoav, James R. Hayden, RBP, Carol Ann Johnson, Bill Jonas, Dwight R. Kuhn, Dr. Dennis Kunkel, Mikki Pet Products, Antonio Philippe, Phototake, Jean Claude Revy, Alice Roche, Dr. Andrew Spielman, Karen Taylor, C. James Webb and Haja van Wessem.

Illustrations by Renée Low.

# HISTORY OF THE

# COCKER SPANIEL

## ANCIENT ORIGINS OF THE DOG

In the beginning, there were wolves and the caveman. Now, just take a look around your neighborhood, the park or any dog show that you might happen to attend. The amazing thing is every breed of dog known to man descends from none other than the "big bad wolf."

How did it all happen? For one thing, it happened very slowly. The transformation actually began in the Mesolithic period of civilization, over 10,000 years ago. There is little doubt that early man saw something of value in the manner in which the wolf pack "sorted out" the herds of animals it pursued. The very young and the geriatric members of a herd were isolated from the healthier, fleet-of-foot individuals.

Obviously, our caveman on his best days wasn't nearly as fast as the wolf when it came to activities of this sort, so he was no doubt impressed by the shrewdness of these fleet four-footed hunters. If nothing else, Mesolithic man recognized that the wolf had some value and, instead of relegating the wolf to mortal-enemy status, he allowed the wolf families to remain unmolested.

As time marched along, some of the wolves became rather friendly with man. Man himself realized he could manipulate breedings of these wolves so that the resulting offspring became somewhat trainable. He began customizing the evolving wolves to suit his growing needs. Although there is no doubt that procuring food remained a top priority on man's list of primary needs, he began assigning other

### ROMAN CLASSIFICATION

As early as the first century AD, Romans had classified dogs into six general groups: House Guardian Dogs, Shepherd Dogs, Sporting Dogs, War Dogs, Scent Dogs and Sight Dogs. Most dogs we know today can trace their ancestry directly back to dogs from these groups. A good many other breeds were developed by combining two or more individuals from these original groups to create yet another "breed."

duties to his friends from the forest: they were becoming hunters, guardians and herders.

From here on, man began to manipulate which animals mated to each other in order to produce an animal that was even more efficient at its respective task. This was the dawning of a new type of wolf, one that we now refer to as *Canis familiaris* (domestic dog) rather than *Canis lupus*.

**ENTER THE HUNTER**
One type of hunting dog that man developed retained the wolf's characteristics of pursuing prey until the prey was cornered and killed, or until the dog was totally exhausted. This practice is more or less typical of the group of dogs known today as hounds. While the tenacity of these trailing dogs was held in high regard, a hound's willingness to chase could continue on for miles if need be, and a good many of the hunters found this counter-

productive to food procurement and, beyond that, wearing on their constitution.

Thus was born the need for a hunting dog that did not follow through on either the chase or the attack. The duty of these close-working hunters was to assist their masters by finding and flushing out or retrieving the game. The dogs worked quietly so as not to scare away the birds and, like any good assistants, they obeyed their master's commands without hesitation. Since the dogs were taken to the hunt in groups, they had to be amiable of disposition and totally non-aggressive with one another.

During the Middle Ages, before guns were invented, hunters used nets and trained hawks to capture their prey. Helping them locate the wild fowl were dogs that actually had originated in Spain—the word *Spain* having its origin in the Latin word *Hispania*. From there, as a natural progression, the word *spaniells* and then the modern word *spaniels* evolved.

At any rate, once these spaniels located the game, some of the dogs would drop to the ground and remain motionless, waiting for the hunter to dash up and fling his net over the covey. These "setting" spaniels later developed into our modern-day Irish, English and Gordon Setters.

Another group of the spaniels

was trained to find birds and drive them out of the underbrush so that falcons could pursue them. These dogs had various names but, for the most part, their names came about as the result of their size at maturity and what they would be used for.

Along with their differences, the spaniels had numerous characteristics in common. Since they most often had to search for their prey through dense shrub and tangled thickets, they needed moderate size, compact bodies and powerful legs to help them move through the difficult terrain that often stopped other breeds cold. They had long silky coats that protected them and easily shed thistles and brambles. Their tails were docked to prevent them from being caught in the brush. They had higher rounded foreheads that are said to have shielded their eyes against branches. Their long lobular ears gathered and channeled scent molecules to their large ultrasensitive noses.

Typical character traits of this group are the dogs' devotion to their owners and their desire to "follow him, even tho they be in a crowd," as it was written at the time. The dogs had merry dispositions and would accompany their masters in the field, "wagging their tails and raising or starting wild game or beasts."

The first spaniel to arrive in

**"THE BARD"**
Although never known to be a dog fancier, "The Bard," William Shakespeare, mentioned spaniels time and time again in his many plays.

the US did so in 1620, arriving on the Mayflower, although no information about this dog is available. Around this time, there were many references to the "spaniells" who had a great talent for springing or flushing birds from their hiding places. Another type within the group was to become known as "cocking spaniells," so named because of their specialty in tracking woodcock.

It was only when dog shows began to become popular in the middle of the 19th century that attempts were made to be more specific in categorizing the spaniels. The first attempt to do so was the creation of separate classifications for land and water

All known spaniels derive from the same background, including the ever-popular English Springer Spaniel, a dog that stands somewhat taller than the Cocker Spaniel.

spaniels. A dividing line of 28 pounds was drawn, with those over the 28-lb limit being classified as Field Spaniels and those falling within the 28-lb limit being classified as Cocker Spaniels (the name being derived from the aforementioned term "cocking spaniells").

Even at that, the lines between the various spaniel breeds were so indistinct that both large and small spaniels were born to the same litter and their ancestry could be comprised of almost anything carrying the spaniel suffix. A perfect example of this confused state of affairs was also one that was to produce the patriarch of the Cocker Spaniel breeds in both America and England. He was born near the end of the 19th century and his name was Obo. He was the black offspring of a Sussex Spaniel sire and a Field Spaniel dam, and bred by Mr. James Farrow in England. Obo, with his fashionable long back and short legs of the day, developed an enviable record at the UK shows. His style and his offspring were very popular, and a number of them were

As efforts were made to distinguish between the types of spaniels, the Cocker was separated from the larger Field Spaniel, shown here, according to weight.

exported to America.

A bitch whose name was Chloe II was bred to Obo in England and sent to the US in whelp. There she produced a litter containing a son that was registered as Obo II. According to the dog authorities of the day, the younger Obo was "not without faults" but still a great stride forward for the breed. He was considered an outstanding sire and by 1920 there was hardly a Cocker in America who did not trace back to him.

It is worth noting that, by this time, the Cocker Spaniel had been registered in the US for over four decades, with registrations tracing back to 1879, even though the breed was not yet recognized as a distinct breed. The first Cocker Spaniel registered was named Captain and was liver and white color.

The red dog Robinhurst Foreglow was whelped in 1917 and traced back to Obo II on both his mother's and father's sides. He was said to be the model Cocker, better than Obo II, with longer legs and a more compact body. He was "more robust in every way and bold and fearless as well," apparently a stylish-looking hunter's companion.

Much the same type as Foreglow was a black descendent named Torohill Trader. Trader was as compact and upstanding as Foreglow but brought what

was thought to be a magnificent headpiece to the breed. His expression truly defined the American ideal of the day.

## FURTHER DIVISION

In America, an interesting and somewhat confusing situation was developing. The Cocker was evolving into two distinct types—one called the American Cocker type and the other called the English Cocker type. Although the latter might have been a bit more streamlined than the Cockers in England, the American fanciers who called their Cockers "English" type believed their dogs to be truer to the type of dog that was bred in England.

The two groups of fanciers had a definite parting of ways, even though both types of dog were registered by the American Kennel Club (AKC) as "Cocker Spaniels." Those who championed the American Cocker type were larger in number and they carried on the trend that had begun with Obo II and Foreglow.

Obo II, credited with founding the breed in the United States, had countless offspring and unprecedented influence on the Cocker Spaniel.

The English Cocker Spaniel (simply called the Cocker Spaniel in the UK) was once considered a "type" of the Cocker breed. Since 1946, the American and English Cockers have been recognized as separate and distinct breeds.

Mrs. Geraldine Rockefeller Dodge receives credit for achieving separate breed status for the American and English types of the Cocker Spaniel.

They favored a Cocker that was proportionately even higher on leg and shorter in back than the old dogs. Torohill Trader was the dog that enabled them to accomplish this.

The group in America who favored the English Cocker type feared that the type they wanted to perpetuate would be lost forever unless drastic steps were taken. In 1936, the English Cocker Spaniel Club of America (ECSCA) was founded and the British standard was adopted as the standard of excellence. The members of the group vowed not to interbreed their dogs with dogs of the American type.

Still, the AKC made no distinction between the Cockers that were registered in its stud book. In order to force the AKC to make a distinction between the two types, the ECSCA realized strong measures had to be taken again. Club president Mrs. Geraldine R. Dodge organized a committee to research the pedi-

grees of all English, American and Canadian Cockers residing in the United States. Then, through a massive pedigree purge, they eliminated any Cocker unable to prove five solid generations of pure English breeding. Only those dogs that could legitimately do so could be identified as pure English Cockers.

## THE AMERICAN VARIETIES

In September 1946, the AKC granted separate breed status to the American and English Cockers, with the English type to be known officially as the English Cocker Spaniel, while the American type was to be called simply the Cocker Spaniel. At the same time, the American type was given three separate varieties: Black, ASCOB (Any Solid Color Other than Black) and Parti-color.

Initially, black and tans were shown in the Parti-color variety. In 1944, they were transferred to the ASCOB variety and, finally, in 1983, they were transferred to the most logical place—the Black variety. It is interesting to note that, in 1948 and again in 1950,

developed. He was beautifully proportioned, and authorities of the day said he was the prototype for the conformation that produced the "reach and drive" so often spoken of in gundogs but so seldom achieved. Trader's influence was so great that it extended to all three of the Cocker varieties, but it is seen so vividly in the Black variety (and in black and tans) that it is worth making special note of.

There is a direct line of descent from Trader that passes down in a direct line to Ch. Elderwood Bangaway, who is

Blue roan is an interesting color that is commonly seen in the English Cocker Spaniel, shown here, but rarely seen in American Cockers.

the parent club for the breed, the American Spaniel Club, asked the AKC to create a separate category for black and tans. This request was not granted.

**BLACKS AND BLACK AND TANS**
There is no doubt that those who hailed Ch. Torohill Trader as the "ideal American Cocker" in the 1930s knew what they were talking about. Not only did Trader help set American type in the breed but he also did so without sacrificing the qualities that made the breed a true flushing spaniel. Trader was a rock-solid dog who had the power and substance that enabled him to perform in the capacity for which spaniels were

In the black and tan, tan points appear above each eye and on the sides of the muzzle and cheeks.

**Jet black is required in the Black variety; a small bit of white on the throat or chest is allowed.**

without a doubt the acknowledged typesetter of the modern black Cocker. He brought elegance, refinement and balance to the breed and was able to pass these traits on to his offspring. His son Ch. DeKarlo's Dashaway and grandsons Ch. Clarkdale Capitol Stock and Ch. Valli-Lo's Flashaway stand behind the top black and black and tan winners in the variety even to this day.

### WIDEST ARRAY OF COLOR
The Cocker Spaniel has one of the widest arrays of acceptable colors and patterns of any breed of dog known to man. Among the possible colors in the Parti-color variety are sable, roan, brown and tan, and blue and white.

## PARTI-COLORS
Parti-colors had great difficulty in keeping up with the advances of the Black variety even though they had descended from what was basically the same stock. One of the most obvious, though not particularly significant, shortcomings of the Parti-color variety was in the wealth of coat commonly found among the Blacks. However, just as soon as it was thought that modernizing the Parti-colors was impossible, Honey Creek Kennels came upon the scene.

The Honey Creek dogs belonged to Bea Wegusen, whose intense linebreeding and inbreeding program completely revolutionized the variety. They won over all Parti-color competition and soon were standing alongside of, if not defeating, the best Blacks being shown. The descendants of Wegusen's top-producing dam, Ch. Honey Creek Vivacious, became the cornerstone of the modern Parti-color variety.

Whatever shortcomings the Honey Creek dogs might have had were rapidly offset by astute breeders who employed the use of solid bloodlines for any needed finishing touches. To this day, it is highly doubtful that even the most modern Parti-color line does not trace back to Honey Creek at some point in its ancestry.

## ASCOBs

The buffs and reds of the ASCOB variety were even slower than the Parti-colors to achieve the level of the Blacks. They seemed destined to remain forever in limbo until the advent of Ch. Maddie's Vagabond's Return in 1950. Here came a modern sporting-type Cocker Spaniel who not only was sound but carried a coat the likes of which had never been seen before among the buffs and reds. Clever breeders of the time used the Vagabond dog well, and as quickly as the first generation came Ch. Gravel Hill Gold Opportunity, a son, who surpassed even his sire in beauty and type. From that point on, the buffs and reds flourished.

The brown (actually liver) Cockers had been around since the days of Obo. However, the color was intensely disliked by the majority of Cocker breeders because dogs of that color were extremely lacking in type and had the glaring yellow eyes that legitimately accompanies the liver color. They were undoubtedly

throwbacks to old Obo, whose sire, it must be remembered, was a liver-colored Sussex Spaniel.

In California, Arline Swalwell of Windridge Kennels was fascinated with the color and decided that she would produce "chocolate" Cockers, as she called them, on a par with those of the other varieties. With the help of Norman Austin and Frances Greer, she set about doing just that.

The trio was joined in its pursuit by two master breeders of the time, Bill Ernst of Begay Cockers and Mike Kinschsular of Lurola fame. Clever use of Black and Parti-color bloodlines so developed the brown Cocker that long-time breeders now consider the work done for the browns one of the most significant advances in the Cocker Spaniel's recent history.

**The buff is perhaps the most commonly seen Cocker color, and without a doubt has attained the quality of the other color varieties.**

**Mepals Rosemary was one of the first Cocker Spaniels to acquire international fame.**

separation of the Cocker Spaniel as a breed in 1946 also came the Cocker's own distinct listing in the AKC's stud book the following January.

The Cocker Spaniel's popularity grew and grew, as did that of the other sporting spaniel breeds. It became impossible for the ASC to put forth equal effort into each of these breeds, and thus it became necessary to transfer certain breeds to other clubs that would become organized into these breeds' respective parent clubs.

Eventually, all of the sporting spaniel breeds except the Cocker were transferred to other parent clubs, with the ASC's retaining jurisdiction over the Cocker Spaniel only. However, the ASC can offer classes for all of the sporting spaniel breeds at its specialty shows. This is truly a unique club, promoting and preserving the best interests of the Cocker Spaniel while retaining dedication to all breeds of sporting spaniel.

*The Parti-color consists of white and another color, and may be in combination with tan points. This is a black and white without tan points.*

## THE AMERICAN SPANIEL CLUB

The American Spaniel Club (ASC) is the parent club of the Cocker Spaniel and was established in 1881, making it older than the AKC itself. The club began to have interest in the Cocker before it even was recognized fully as a separate breed. The ASC became a member club of the American Kennel Club as the parent club of the sporting spaniel breeds. With the official

### THREE VARIETIES

Each of the three varieties of Cocker Spaniel (Black, ASCOB and Parti-color) are shown separately and the winners of each variety go on to compete in the Sporting Group.

**ONE OF AMERICA'S TOP DOGS!**
The Cocker Spaniel is the smallest of the sporting spaniels and is one of the most popular pure-bred dogs in the United States. Many Americans know him as a companion dog, and his adaptability and love of his human family make his popularity in this respect well-deserved. Of course, a Cocker in the show ring, gaiting confidently in full coat, is a magnificent sight.

One should not, however, forget the Cocker's origins as a sporting dog and hunter's able assistant; he is a spaniel, after all! These skills should not be lost in today's Cockers. When trained properly, they still perform as gun dogs, flushing game and retrieving when commanded. Likewise, the breed's inherent talents make it an excellent all-around competitor. The Cocker is successful in the conformation ring, as well as in performance events like obedience and field trials. The Cocker Spaniel breed boasts many Dual and Triple Champions, proving that this is a dog that has it all...brains, brawn and beauty!

From coast to coast and on both sides of the Atlantic, the Cocker Spaniel is a swimming success!

# CHARACTERISTICS OF THE

# COCKER SPANIEL

**Though not a retrieving breed by nature, one of the Cocker's tasks as a hunting assistant is to retrieve from the water when the need arises.**

Diehard Sporting-dog enthusiasts have been a bit unfair in their criticism of the Cocker Spaniel, even suggesting that the modern Cocker is no longer a dog suitable for hunting and that it should be moved to another group for competition at dog shows. The criticism stems primarily from the excessive amount of feathering that the modern show Cocker Spaniel carries.

Since most Cocker puppies purchased in this day and age are bred in kennels whose ultimate goal is to breed show dogs, it must be said that the entire breed is now one that must be classed in the extremely heavy-coated category. However, what must be determined is whether or not the hair on the outside of the dog changes what exists inside the dog.

Another of the anti-coat contingent's arguments is that the show Cocker Spaniel is rarely, if ever, seen in the field today. This may well be true, but again, one can only wonder just how many of today's Irish Setter or Pointer show dogs are used in the field? Relatively few would be my best guess, and yet there has been no call to remove these and other

## LONGEST LIFESPAN
The Cocker Spaniel has one of the longest lifespans of the many Sporting breeds.

**JACK OF ALL TRADES**
The Cocker Spaniel has been highly successful in just about every pursuit available to purebred dogs, including conformation show competition, field work and trials, obedience trials, therapy work and assistance work for the infirmed.

seldom-seen-in-the-field dogs from the Sporting Group.

Maintaining a Cocker in full show coat is undoubtedly a task requiring a great deal of time and ability. However, electric clippers and a pair of thinning shears can very quickly reveal what is under all of that hair. Once clipped down, I find the Cocker is no less a sturdy little gundog than he was in the beginning. I have known many owners who have taken their Cockers out into the field on a lark and have quickly been made aware that the thing lacking most in the Cocker's ability to work in the field is the opportunity to do so.

Under the obvious wealth of furnishings, a well-bred Cocker Spaniel remains a most versatile companion. He is small enough to make a pleasant house dog, yet of more than sufficient size and stamina to spend the day trudging alongside his master over hill and dale. When you do your trudging, just make sure that your Cocker

companion is under control at all times, because the first bunny that pops up or the first waterfowl that takes off across the pond will find your bob-tailed friend in hot pursuit!

Before dashing out to purchase a Cocker—in fact, before thinking about buying any dog—a person should definitely sit down and think the prospect out thoroughly. Little Cocker puppies snuggled together and fast asleep one on top of the other are absolutely irresistible, I assure you. Why else would you see them so often gracing greeting cards or on calendars in all parts of the world? The breed's photogenic little faces are a good part of what encourages well-meaning but misguided individuals to dash out to buy a puppy for themselves or as a gift for loved ones.

This is not to say that the

One look at these precious faces and it's easy to understand the Cocker pup's undeniable appeal.

**MERRY TEMPERAMENT**
The well-bred Cocker Spaniel has an exceptionally calm nature and, though his temperament is certainly merry, he is not high-strung and seldom barks without good reason.

Puppies don't come pre-educated...at least not the puppies I have known. Everything you think a well-behaved dog should know how to do will have to be taught to him by you, his master and owner. Cockers learn quickly, but no more quickly or more slowly than most other breeds. It all takes time, and the question you must ask yourself is whether or not you have the time to devote to this education.

Above all, it is important to ask if the person who will ultimately be responsible for the dog's day-to-day care really wants a dog. If that person is you, you will have the answer. All too often, it seems that the responsibility of caring for the family dog often ends up falling on one person once the novelty of bringing the new pup home wears off. This may not come about intentionally, but it's a familiar story as everyone in the family is busy with work, school, activities and so on.

Of course, no one wants to stand by and watch any creature be neglected. Thus, someone has to take the dog to the vet, rush out to buy the dog food and take the dog out for a walk, among other duties. No matter how busy you and the members of your family are, you will have to make time for these additional tasks once a dog enters the picture.

Pet care can be an excellent

pudgy little ball of fluff you bring home will not duplicate those angelic greeting card poses on occasion. The operative words here, however, are "on occasion." Real puppies spend their days investigating, digging, chewing, eating, relieving themselves, needing to go outdoors, etc., all things requiring an owner's time and vigilant attention.

way to teach children responsibility once they've reached an appropriate age, but it should be understood that, in their enthusiasm to have a puppy, children will promise just about anything. It is what will happen after the novelty of owning a new dog has worn off that must be considered.

Then too, even if Mom and Dad have given their OK on a puppy, does the lifestyle and schedule of the household lend itself to the demands of proper dog care? Don't forget, there must always be someone available to see to a dog's basic needs: feeding, exercise, coat care, access to the outdoors when required and so on. If you or your family is gone from morning to night or if you travel frequently and are away from home for long periods of time, the dog still must be cared for. Will someone willingly be present to do so, or are you prepared to pay the costs of frequent boarding-kennel housing for your dog while you are gone?

You must also stop to think about the suitability of the Cocker for the household, whether "household" means half a dozen children and adults or just you. Toy breeds are not suitable for toddlers. Very young children can be very rough and unintentionally hurt a small puppy. It also takes a lot of explaining to convince very young children that a Cocker's ears are not "handles." On the

other hand, a young puppy of any breed can overwhelm and sometimes injure an infant or small child in an enthusiastic moment.

## IS A COCKER THE RIGHT DOG FOR ME?

The entire history of the Cocker has been one of constant and close association with people. Whether in the field or home at the hearth, the Cocker lives to be with his owner. Of the many breeds that we have owned and bred, I can honestly say that the well-bred Cocker is one of the most amiable. The breed can be equally comfortable with children and the elderly. Cocker Spaniels

Learning to care for a Cocker puppy can be a way to teach children about responsibility, provided that the children are old enough and are willing to take on the considerable effort involved.

are compatible with breeds much larger than themselves as well as the tiniest of Toy breeds. Introduced early enough, even a cat can be a Cocker's friend and companion.

The Cocker in full show coat may look too artificial to cope with day-to-day life, but that look is entirely deceiving. Under that coat is a sturdy, agile and sound little dog that is constructed to be able to keep up easily with the most active youngster or adult.

A Cocker is always ready for a good romp, a long hike or a jog in the park. Sensibly-bred Cockers are neither hyperactive nor overly excitable. The Cocker is more than happy to spend a quiet afternoon or evening with an owner who wants to do nothing more than read a book or listen to music. On the other hand, the same dog will gladly accept an invitation to climb the hills or run the beach with equal enthusiasm.

The Cocker Spaniel is a built-in alarm system, but not one that is set off without good reason. The breed is very protective of its home and territory and will sound the alarm when necessary, but a Cocker does not find it necessary to react to every situation he observes with hysterical barking.

**GROOMING CONSIDERATIONS**

As amiable a breed as the Cocker is, there are other criteria to be considered before setting your heart on the breed. The freshly bathed and groomed Cocker in full coat certainly presents a beautiful picture, but a Cocker enjoys digging holes and traipsing through mud puddles as much as any other dog. The full-length show coat requires a tremendous amount of bathing, trimming, grooming and, yes, house-cleaning.

A good part of all that work can be eliminated by keeping your Cocker in what might be called a pet or utility clip. This will require you either to learn how to do this yourself or to employ the services of a professional groomer. With time, practice and the right grooming tools, the art can be mastered.

Yes, a Cocker can have a feline friend! These two take over their owner's armchair for a little relaxation.

## MALE OR FEMALE?

While some individuals may have personal preferences about the sex of their dog, I can honestly say that both the male and the female Cocker are equal in their trainability and affection. The decision will have more to do with the lifestyle and ultimate plans of the owner than with differences between the sexes in the breed.

There is one point that the prospective buyer should consider. While both the male and female Cocker must be trained not to urinate in the home, the male does provide an additional problem. The male of any breed of dog has a natural instinct to lift his leg and urinate on objects to establish and "mark" his territory. The degree of effort that must be invested in training the male not to do this varies with the individual dog. This habit becomes increasingly more difficult to correct with the number of times a male dog is used for breeding. The mating act increases his need and desire to mark his territory.

On the other hand, one must realize that the female will have her semi-annual and sometimes burdensome heat cycles after she is eight or nine months old. At these times, she must be confined to prevent her from soiling her surroundings. She must also be closely watched to prevent male dogs from gaining access to her or else she will become pregnant.

A Cocker Spaniel in full show coat. Having your Cocker look like this requires professional assistance until you learn to groom and maintain the coat yourself.

Both the male's and female's sexually related problems can be eliminated by having the pet Cocker "altered." Spaying the female and neutering the male will not change the character of your pet but will avoid the problems you will have to contend with in sexually entire dogs. Neutering also precludes the possibility of your pet's adding to the extreme pet overpopulation problem that concerns environmentalists worldwide. Most vets and breeders recommend altering dogs that are not intended for showing or breeding, as it helps to lessen or eliminate the possibility of certain health problems, including cancers.

It is important to understand that the procedures to alter a dog,

The pet trim is much easier to maintain if your Cocker is not a show dog. The pet Cocker's coat is still beautiful at a shorter length.

the Cocker puppy you purchase comes from a source where physical and mental soundness are primary considerations in the breeding program. Achieving this goal is usually the result of careful breeding over a period of many years. Selective breeding is aimed at maintaining the virtues of the breed and eliminating genetic weaknesses. Because this selective breeding is time-consuming and costly, good breeders protect their investment by providing the best prenatal care for their breeding females and the best nutrition for the growing puppies. There is no substitute for the amount of dedication and care that good breeders give to their dogs.

This is not to imply that your Cocker puppy must come from a large kennel. On the contrary, many good puppies are produced by small hobby breeders in their homes. These names may well be included in recommendations from the American Kennel Club, the American Spaniel Club and local or regional breed clubs. These individuals should offer the same investment of time, study and knowledge as the larger kennels and they should be just as ready to stand behind their puppies' health and temperaments.

male or female, are not reversible. If you are considering the possibility of showing your Cocker, altered animals are not allowed to compete in conformation dog shows. Altered animals may, however, compete in obedience trials, agility events, field trials and other performance events.

**WHERE TO BUY YOUR COCKER**
Your Cocker will live with you for many years. It is not at all surprising to see Cockers live to be 10, 12 and often 15 years of age. It is therefore extremely important that

**HEALTH CONSIDERATIONS**
In the wild, any genetically transferred infirmity that would inter-

fere with a newborn animal's survival would automatically be eliminated from the gene pool. Inability to nurse, to capture food as an adult or to escape from a predator are obviously impairments that would shorten any animal's life very quickly. We who control the breeding of our domesticated dogs are intent upon saving all the puppies in a litter, but, in preserving life, we also perpetuate health problems. Our humanitarian proclivities thus have a downside as well.

Generally speaking, the Cocker Spaniel is a healthy breed, often living to be 14 or 15 years of age. However, as careful as long-time Cocker breeders might be in the stock they choose for their breeding programs, hereditary problems still occur. Like all other breeds of domesticated dog, Cockers have their share of hereditary problems.

The following represent problems that do exist in the breed. This does not mean that the puppy you buy or the line from which your pup comes will necessarily be afflicted with any of the genetic disorders described herein, but they should be discussed with the breeder from whom you purchase your dog. The reputable breeder will have all of his breeding stock tested and will eliminate from his program all dogs that test positive for any hereditary problems.

## DOGS, DOGS, GOOD FOR YOUR HEART!

People usually purchase dogs for companionship, but studies show that dogs can help to improve their owners' health and level of activity, as well as lower a human's risk of coronary heart disease. Without even realizing it, when a person puts time into exercising, grooming and feeding a dog, he also puts more time into his own personal health care. Dog owners establish more routine schedules for their dogs to follow, which can have positive effects on their own health. Dogs also teach us patience, offer unconditional love and provide the joy of having a furry friend to pet!

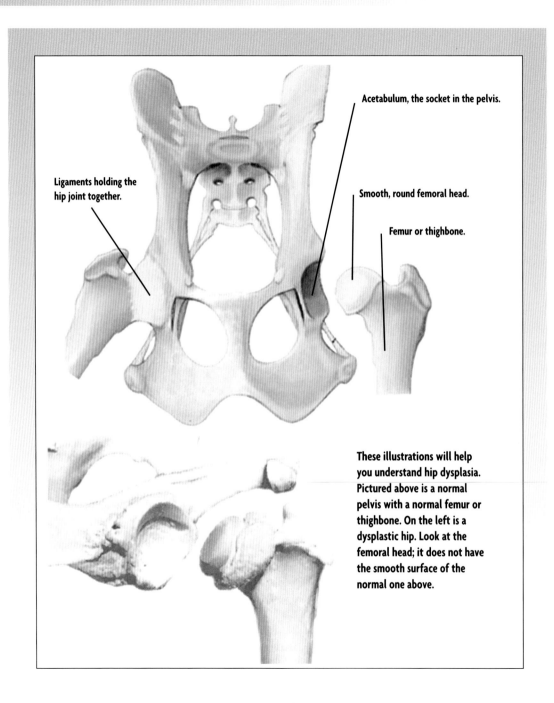

Acetabulum, the socket in the pelvis.

Ligaments holding the hip joint together.

Smooth, round femoral head.

Femur or thighbone.

These illustrations will help you understand hip dysplasia. Pictured above is a normal pelvis with a normal femur or thighbone. On the left is a dysplastic hip. Look at the femoral head; it does not have the smooth surface of the normal one above.

Likewise, the reputable Cocker breeder is aware of the following problems and should be willing to discuss them with you.

## EYE PROBLEMS

There are three eye conditions that have been designated as hereditary in the Cocker Spaniel. They are heritable cataracts (HC), progressive retinal atrophy (PRA) and retinal dysplasia (RD). All of these conditions can be diagnosed by an experienced veterinary ophthalmologist.

**Cataracts:** A condition of the eye in which the lens appears milky or opaque. Appearance of hereditary cataracts may occur as early as puppyhood (referred to as juvenile cataracts) or may not occur until later in the dog's life. Cataracts can affect one or both eyes and their effect can range from partial to total blindness.

**Progressive Retinal Atrophy:** Generally referred to as night blindness, PRA is a condition of the retina that at first may seem temporary or that creates slight impairment of night vision. However, the condition continually develops and eventually leads to total blindness.

**Retinal Dysplasia:** This condition is the result of abnormal development of the layers of the retina. This cause of blindness can occur in very young puppies as well as in adults.

**Cherry Eye:** The term is commonly used to describe a condition in which the lymph gland of the third eyelid becomes enlarged through an infection or allergy. It bulges out in the corner of the eye closest to the nose. In some cases, it can be treated by a veterinarian or it may be surgically removed.

## SKELETAL PROBLEMS

**Patellar Luxation (Slipped Stifles):** The condition can be found in one or both knees of the Cocker. The ligament that holds the patella (kneecap) in place can be so weak that it slips from the groove in which it would normally fit to bind the upper and lower thigh together. It can be painful and can cause limping in some cases.

**Hip Dysplasia (HD):** Hip dysplasia is a condition in which the ball and socket arrangement of the hip and upper femur is so poorly developed that the femur rotates within the socket. Depending upon the severity of the condition, hip dysplasia can cause stiffness, limping and even total paralysis of the rear quarters.

**Factor X (Factor 10):** This is a hereditary blood coagulation defect. Blood clotting is a complex process that requires a minimum of 13 different clotting proteins. Deficiency in any one of them can result in a blood-clotting disorder. Factor X represents a deficiency in just one of these proteins.

# COCKER SPANIEL

The Cocker Spaniel with the right construction, shape, balance and proportion is a beautiful sight to behold. The question arises, however: What is it that tells us if a Cocker Spaniel does in fact have "the right construction, shape, balance and proportion?" Wouldn't the opinion of one person be just as valid as the next?

The answers to this question are found in the American Kennel Club's breed standard. Breed standards are very accurate descriptions of the ideal specimen of a given breed. A breed standard describes an ideal member of the given breed physically—listing all of a breed's anatomical parts and telling how those parts should

The long feathering on the Cocker's ears is wrapped and protected until the dog appears in the ring. While the breed's glorious coat is maintained meticulously, it must never serve to cover conformational flaws.

look. The standard also describes the breed's temperament and how the dog should move.

This standard is the blueprint that breeders use to fashion their breeding programs. The goal, of course, is to move one step closer to that ever-elusive picture of perfection with each succeeding generation. The breed standard is also what dog show judges use to evaluate which of the dogs being shown compares most favorably to what is required.

It should be understood that what the standard describes is the perfect dog of a given breed. In nature, nothing is absolutely perfect. Thus, the breeder and the judge are looking for the dog that in their opinion has "most of the best." How each individual person interprets this will always vary somewhat, but there is usually little disagreement when a dog comes along that truly has most of what the breed standard actually asks for. No dog will have it all.

Although it takes many years to fully understand the implications of a breed standard, it behooves the prospective owner of any breed to familiarize himself with the requirements. This will enable the person who wishes to own a dog of that breed to have a good idea of what a quality specimen should look and act like.

## THE AMERICAN KENNEL CLUB BREED STANDARD FOR THE COCKER SPANIEL

**General Appearance:** The Cocker Spaniel is the smallest member of the Sporting Group. He has a sturdy, compact body and a cleanly chiseled and refined head, with the overall dog in complete balance and of ideal size. He stands well up at the shoulder on straight forelegs with a topline sloping slightly toward strong, moderately bent, muscular quarters. He is a dog capable of considerable speed, combined with great endurance. Above all, he must be free and merry, sound, well balanced throughout and in action show a keen inclination to work. A dog well balanced in all parts is more desirable than a dog with strongly contrasting good points and faults.

**Size, Proportion, Substance:** *Size*—The ideal height at the withers for an adult dog is 15 inches and for an adult bitch, 14 inches. Height may vary one-half inch above or below this ideal. A dog whose height exceeds 15.5 inches or a bitch whose height exceeds 14.5 inches shall be disqualified. An

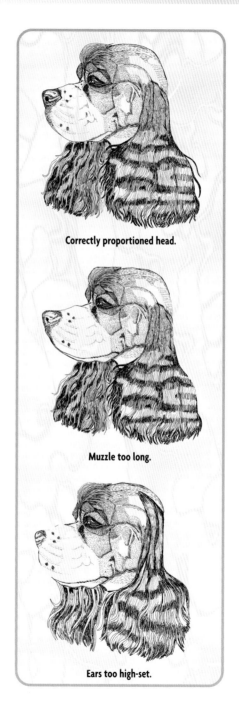

Correctly proportioned head.

Muzzle too long.

Ears too high-set.

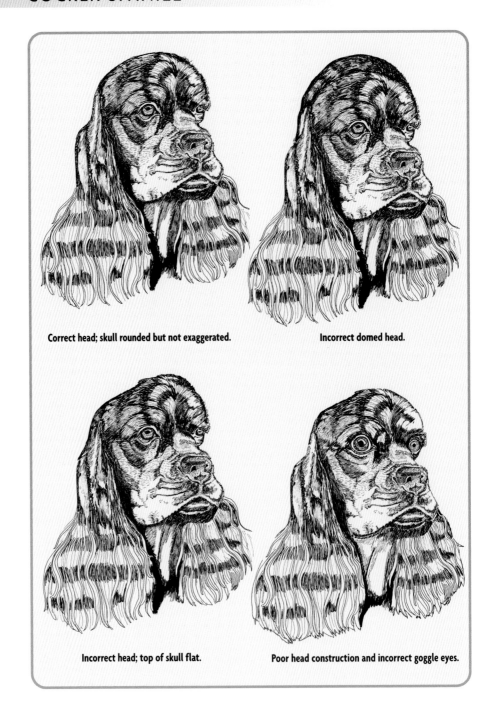

Correct head; skull rounded but not exaggerated.

Incorrect domed head.

Incorrect head; top of skull flat.

Poor head construction and incorrect goggle eyes.

adult dog whose height is less than 14.5 inches and an adult bitch whose height is less than 13.5 inches shall be penalized. Height is determined by a line perpendicular to the ground from the top of the shoulder blades, the dog standing naturally with its forelegs and lower hind legs parallel to the line of measurement. *Proportion*—The measurement from the breast bone to back of thigh is slightly longer than the measurement from the highest point of withers to the ground. The body must be of sufficient length to permit a straight and free stride; the dog never appears long and low.

**Head:** To attain a well proportioned head, which must be in balance with the rest of the dog, it embodies the following: *Expression*—The expression is intelligent, alert, soft and appealing. *Eyes*—Eyeballs are round and full and look directly forward. The shape of the eye rims gives a slightly almond shaped appearance; the eye is not weak or goggled. The color of the iris is dark brown and in general the darker the better. *Ears*—Lobular, long, of fine leather, well feathered, and placed no higher than a line to the lower part of the eye. *Skull*— Rounded but not exaggerated with no tendency toward flatness; the eyebrows are clearly defined with a pronounced stop. The bony structure beneath the eyes is well chiseled with no prominence in the

cheeks. The muzzle is broad and deep, with square even jaws. To be in correct balance, the distance from the stop to the tip of the nose is one half the distance from the stop up over the crown to the base

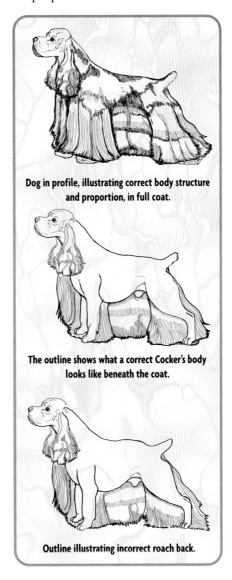

Dog in profile, illustrating correct body structure and proportion, in full coat.

The outline shows what a correct Cocker's body looks like beneath the coat.

Outline illustrating incorrect roach back.

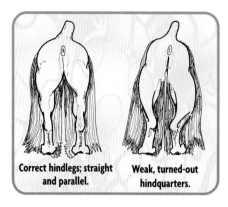

Correct hindlegs; straight and parallel.    Weak, turned-out hindquarters.

of the skull. *Nose*—Of sufficient size to balance the muzzle and foreface, with well developed nostrils typical of a sporting dog. It is black in color in the blacks, black and tans, and black and whites; in other colors it may be brown, liver or black, the darker the better. The color of nose harmonizes with the color of the eye rim. *Lips*—The upper lip is full and of sufficient depth to cover the lower jaw. *Teeth*—Teeth strong and sound, not too small and meet in a scissors bite.

**Neck, Topline, Body:** *Neck*—The neck is sufficiently long to allow the nose to reach the ground easily, muscular and free from pendulous "throatiness." It rises strongly from the shoulders and arches slightly as it tapers to join the head. *Topline*—sloping slightly toward muscular quarters. *Body*—The chest is deep, its lowest point no higher than the elbows, its front sufficiently wide for adequate heart and lung space,

yet not so wide as to interfere with the straightforward movement of the forelegs. Ribs are deep and well sprung. Back is strong and sloping evenly and slightly downward from the shoulders to the set-on of the docked tail. The docked tail is set on and carried on a line with the topline of the back, or slightly higher; never straight up like a Terrier and never so low as to indicate timidity. When the dog is in motion the tail action is merry.

**Forequarters:** The shoulders are well laid back forming an angle with the upper arm of approximately 90 degrees which permits the dog to move his forelegs in an easy manner with forward reach. Shoulders are clean-cut and sloping without protrusion and so set that the upper points of the withers are at an angle which permits a wide spring of rib. When viewed from the side with the forelegs vertical, the elbow is directly below the highest point of the shoulder blade. Forelegs are parallel, straight, strongly boned and muscular and set close to the body well under the scapulae. The pasterns are short and strong. Dewclaws on forelegs may be removed. Feet compact, large, round and firm with horny pads; they turn neither in nor out.

**Hindquarters:** Hips are wide and quarters well rounded and muscular. When viewed from behind, the hind legs are parallel when in motion and at rest. The hind legs are strongly boned, and muscled with moderate angulation at the stifle and powerful, clearly defined thighs. The stifle is strong and there is no slippage of it in motion or when standing. The hocks are strong and well let down. Dewclaws on hind legs may be removed.

**Coat:** On the head, short and fine; on the body, medium length, with enough undercoating to give protection. The ears, chest, abdomen and legs are well feathered, but not so excessively as to hide the Cocker Spaniel's true lines and movement or affect his appearance and function as a moderately coated sporting dog. The texture is most important. The coat is silky, flat or slightly wavy and of a texture which permits easy care. Excessive coat or curly or cottony textured coat shall be severely penalized. Use of electric clippers on the back coat is not desirable. Trimming to enhance the dog's true lines should be done to appear as natural as possible.

**Color and Markings:** *Black Variety*—Solid color black to include black with tan points. The black should be jet; shadings of brown or liver in the coat are not desirable. A small amount of white on the chest and/or throat is allowed; white in any other loca-

tion shall disqualify. *Any Solid Color Other than Black (ASCOB)*—Any solid color other than black, ranging from lightest cream to darkest red, including brown and brown with tan points. The color shall be of a uniform shade, but lighter color of the feathering is permissible. A small amount of white on the chest and/or throat is allowed; white in any other location shall disqualify. *Parti-Color Variety*—Two or more solid, well broken colors, one of which must be white; black and white, red and white (the red may range from lightest cream to darkest red), brown and white, and roans, to include any such color combination with tan points. It is preferable that the tan markings be located in the same pattern as for the tan points in the Black and ASCOB varieties. Roans are classified as

Remember that the Cocker Spaniel is a sporting dog and must possess the ability to move like one. Despite his small size, the Cocker has a ground-covering gait, powered by strong front reach and rear drive.

parti-colors and may be of any of the usual roaning patterns. Primary color which is ninety percent (90%) or more shall disqualify. *Tan Points*—The color of the tan may be from the lightest cream to the darkest red and is restricted to ten percent (10%) or less of the color of the specimen; tan markings in excess of that amount shall disqualify. In the case of tan points in the Black or ASCOB variety, the markings shall be located as follows:

1) A clear tan spot over each eye;
2) On the sides of the muzzle and on the cheeks;
3) On the underside of the ears;
4) On all feet and/or legs;
5) Under the tail;
6) On the chest, optional; presence or absence shall not be penalized.

Tan markings which are not readily visible or which amount only to traces shall be penalized. Tan on the muzzle which extends upward, over and joins shall also be penalized. The absence of tan markings in the Black or ASCOB variety in any of the specified locations in any otherwise tan-pointed dog shall disqualify.

**Gait:** The Cocker Spaniel, though the smallest of the sporting dogs, possesses a typical sporting dog gait. Prerequisite to good movement is balance between the front and rear assemblies. He drives with strong, powerful rear quarters and is properly constructed in the shoulders and forelegs so that he can reach forward without constriction in a full stride to counterbalance the driving force from the rear. Above all, his gait is coordinated, smooth and effortless. The dog must cover ground with his action; excessive animation should not be mistaken for proper gait.

**Temperament:** Equable in temperament with no suggestion of timidity.

**Disqualifications:**
*Height*—Males over 15.5 inches; females over 14.5 inches.
*Color and Markings*—The aforementioned colors are the only acceptable colors or combination of colors. Any other colors or combination of colors to disqualify.
*Black Variety*—White markings except on chest and throat.
*Any Solid Color Other Than Black Variety*—White markings except on chest and throat.
*Parti-color Variety*—Primary color ninety percent (90%) or more.
*Tan Points*—(1) Tan markings in excess of ten percent (10%); (2) Absence of tan markings in Black or ASCOB Variety in any of the specified locations in an otherwise tan pointed dog.

**Approved May 12, 1992**
**Effective June 30, 1992**

# COCKER SPANIEL

## ARE YOU READY FOR A COCKER SPANIEL?

Have you ever been to the home of a friend or relative who owned an unruly dog? This untrained, attention-starved creature hurls himself at company, climbing up on your lap, mounting your leg and the like. Of course, the owner does not seem to notice, and has no means to discipline or control the animal. A nuisance, to say the least!

You must make a very careful decision here. Do you really want the responsibility of owning and training a Cocker Spaniel? He is an animal who needs your companionship and attention. He is very smart, but needs your patience and dedication to his training to get your message across. A primary consideration is time—not only the time of the dog's expected lifespan, which can be well over 10 or 12 years, but also the time required each day to care for the little fellow. If you are not committed to providing for the welfare of this energetic and heavily coated animal; if, in the simplest, most basic example, you are not willing to walk your Cocker Spaniel daily, despite the weather, do not choose a Cocker as a companion.

Safe living quarters and adequate space for the dog to stretch his legs are additional considerations for Cocker ownership. When the Cocker is a baby, a space the size of an infant's play-pen is all that is required, but once your Cocker begins to grow, far more space will be needed. A fenced yard or secure kennel run is an absolute must.

In addition, there are the usual problems associated with puppies of any breed, like the damages likely to be sustained by your floors, furniture and flowers,

### INHERIT THE MIND

In order to know whether or not a puppy will fit into your lifestyle, you need to assess his personality. A good way to do this is to interact with his parents. Your pup inherits not only his appearance but also his personality and temperament from the sire and dam. If the parents are fearful or overly aggressive, these same traits may likely show up in your puppy.

### TIME TO GO HOME

Breeders rarely release puppies until they are eight to ten weeks of age. This is an acceptable age for most breeds of dog, excepting toy breeds, which are not released until around 12 weeks, given their petite sizes. If a breeder has a puppy that is 12 weeks of age or older, it is likely well social-ized and house-trained. Be sure that it is otherwise healthy before deciding to take it home.

and, not least of all, restrictions to your freedom (of movement) as in vacations or weekend trips. This union is a serious affair and should be deeply considered.

The acquisition of any dog should be a carefully considered decision. All members of the family should share in the selection and care of the puppy.

Once decided, though, your choice of a Cocker Spaniel can be the most rewarding of all breeds.

### BUYING A COCKER SPANIEL PUPPY

Most likely you are seeking a Cocker Spaniel that is destined to be a pet and not necessarily a show dog. That does not mean you are looking for a second-rate puppy. A "pet-quality" Cocker, as a dog that is not suitable for showing or breeding is often called, is not like a used car or a "slightly irregular" shirt. Your pet must be as sound, healthy and temperamentally fit as any top show dog. Pet owners do not want Cockers that aren't sound of both body and mind, that aren't trustworthy and reliable around children and strangers and that don't look like Cocker Spaniels. Even if not buying a show or field dog, you still want a Cocker Spaniel—a smart little gundog with the melting spaniel expres-sion, sound hips, good eyes and a lovable personality. If these quali-ties are not important to you as a Cocker Spaniel owner, then you must ask yourself why you are interested in the breed at all.

The safest method of obtain-ing your new Cocker puppy is to seek out a reputable breeder. This is suggested even if you are not looking for a show specimen. The novice breeders and pet owners who advertise at attractive prices in the local newspapers are probably kind enough towards their dogs, but may not have the facilities or experience required to successfully raise these animals.

National clubs like the AKC and the ASC, as well as local and regional Cocker clubs, can refer you to breeders and other contacts within the breed. Clubs require their member breeders to follow strict codes of ethics in their breeding programs.

Once you've contacted some breeders, you can begin visiting potentially suitable litters. Spend time watching the pups and talking to the breeders. Inquire about inoculations and when the puppy was last dosed for worms. Check the ears for any signs of mites or irritation. Are the eyes clear and free of any debris? The puppy coat is softer, fluffier and shorter than the adult coat and should feel silky and clean to the touch. The Cocker comes in a variety of

A good place to make contacts in the breed who can point you in the right direction to finding a puppy is a dog show. Talking to the handlers when they are not busy and meeting the breeders of the dogs you like are excellent ways to gain helpful information.

colors and, if dog shows are not in your dog's future, the color variety that appeals most to you is the one you should choose.

Never settle for anything less than a happy, healthy, outgoing puppy. A Cocker puppy should love the world and everyone in it. As playful as the puppy might be, he should not object to being held. Cocker puppies that squirm and struggle to be released have probably not had proper socialization or might have inherited antisocial behavior.

## PUPPY APPEARANCE

Your puppy should have a well-fed appearance but not a distended abdomen, which may indicate worms or incorrect feeding, or both. The body should be firm, with a solid feel. The skin of the abdomen should be pale pink and clean, without signs of scratching or rash. Check the legs to see if the dewclaws were removed, as breeders usually have this done when the pups are a few days old.

The head of the Cocker Spaniel is the most distinctive and unique of all the spaniels because of the breed's velvety, melting expression. Large, luminous and dark eyes are a must for the breed. Eyes must not be running or sensitive to light.

Check the pup's mouth to make sure that the bite is fairly even. Maturity can correct minor errors in dentition that are present at puppyhood, but never select a puppy that has any deformities of the mouth or jaw.

Pay attention to the way your selection moves. The Cocker Spaniel in puppyhood (particularly around eight weeks) is a miniaturized replica of what he looks like at maturity. Seek the puppy that is short and stylish-looking with sound, deliberate movement. There should be no inclination to stumble or limp. Do realize that the chubby little boy puppies might be a bit more awkward than their svelte sisters, so do make allowances.

One last golden rule to emphasize: A merry and loving temperament above all is the hallmark of the spaniel family. Do not settle for anything less!

**COMMITMENT OF OWNERSHIP**
After considering all of these factors, you have most likely already made some very important decisions about selecting your puppy. You have chosen the

**THE COCOA WARS**

Chocolate contains the chemical thebromine, which is poisonous to dogs, although "chocolates" especially made for dogs are safe (as they don't actually contain chocolate) but not recommended. Any item that encourages your dog to enjoy the taste of cocoa should be discouraged. You should also exercise caution when using mulch in your yard. This frequently contains cocoa hulls, and dogs have been known to die from eating the mulch.

help you learn to recognize certain behavior and to determine what a pup's behavior indicates about his temperament. You will be able to pick out which pups are the leaders, which ones are less outgoing, which ones are confident, which ones are shy, playful, friendly, aggressive, etc. Equally as important, you will learn to recognize what a *healthy* pup should look and act like. All of these things will help you in your search, and when you find

Cocker Spaniel, which means that you have decided which characteristics you want in a dog and what type of dog will best fit into your family and lifestyle. If you have selected a breeder, you have gone a step further—you have done your research and found a responsible, conscientious person who breeds quality Cockers and who should be a reliable source of help as you and your puppy adjust to life together. If you have observed a litter in action, you have obtained a firsthand look at the dynamics of a puppy "pack" and, thus, you should have learned about each pup's individual personality—perhaps you have even found one that particularly appeals to you.

However, even if you have not yet found the Cocker puppy of your dreams, observing pups will

The Cocker puppy that you want is a friendly, alert, healthy little spaniel with an expression to melt your heart.

the Cocker Spaniel that was meant for you, you will know it!

Researching your breed, selecting a responsible breeder and observing as many pups as possible are all important steps on the way to dog ownership. It may seem like a lot of effort…and you have not even taken the pup

home yet! Remember, though, you cannot be too careful when it comes to deciding on the type of dog you want and finding out about your prospective pup's background. Buying a puppy is not—or *should* not be—just another whimsical purchase. This is one instance in which you actually do get to choose your own family! You may be thinking that buying a puppy should be fun—it should not be so serious and so much work. Keep in mind that your puppy is not a cuddly stuffed toy or decorative lawn ornament, but a creature that will become a real member of your

### PEDIGREE VS. REGISTRATION CERTIFICATE

Too often new owners are confused between these two important documents. Your puppy's pedigree, essentially a family tree, is a written record of a dog's genealogy of three generations or more. The pedigree will show you the names as well as performance titles of all the dogs in your pup's background. Your breeder must provide you with a registration application, with his part properly filled out. You must complete the application and send it to the AKC with the proper fee. Every puppy must come from a litter that has been AKC-registered by the breeder, born in the USA and from a sire and dam that are also registered with the AKC.

The seller must provide you with complete records to identify the puppy. The AKC requires that the seller provide the buyer with the following: breed; sex, color and markings; date of birth; litter number (when available); names and registration numbers of the parents; breeder's name; and date sold or delivered.

family. You will come to realize that, while buying a puppy is a pleasurable and exciting endeavor, it is not something to be taken lightly. Relax…the fun will start when the pup comes home!

Always keep in mind that a puppy is nothing more than a baby in a furry disguise…a baby who is virtually helpless in a human world and who trusts his owner for fulfillment of his basic needs for survival. In addition to food, water and shelter, your pup needs care, protection, guidance and love. If you are not prepared to commit to this, then you are not prepared to own a dog.

"Wait a minute," you say. "How hard could this be? All of my neighbors own dogs and they seem to be doing just fine. Why should I have to worry about all of this?" Well, you should not worry about it; in fact, you will probably find that once your Cocker pup gets used to his new home, he will fall into his place

**ARE YOU PREPARED?**
Unfortunately, when a puppy is bought by someone who does not take into consideration the time and attention that dog ownership requires, it is the puppy who suffers when he is either abandoned or placed in a shelter by a frustrated owner. So all of the "homework" you do in preparation for your pup's arrival will benefit you both. The more informed you are, the more you will know what to expect and the better equipped you will be to handle the ups and downs of raising a puppy. Hopefully, everyone in the household is willing to do his part in raising and caring for the pup. The anticipation of owning a dog often brings a lot of promises from excited family members: "I will walk him every day," "I will feed him," "I will house-train him," etc., but these things take time and effort, and promises can easily be forgotten once the novelty of the new pet has worn off.

How will you be able to choose from all of those adorable faces? The breeder will be an invaluable source of help in guiding you to the pup whose personality will best match your lifestyle.

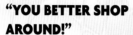

**"YOU BETTER SHOP AROUND!"**

Finding a reputable breeder who sells healthy pups is very important, but make sure that the breeder you choose is not only someone you respect but also someone with whom you feel comfortable. Your breeder will be a resource long after you buy your puppy, and you must be able to call with reasonable questions without being made to feel like a pest! If you don't connect on a personal level, investigate some other breeders before making a final decision.

in the family quite naturally. But it never hurts to emphasize the commitment of dog ownership. With some time and patience, it is really not too difficult to raise a curious and exuberant Cocker Spaniel pup to be a well-adjusted and well-mannered adult dog—a dog that could be your most loyal friend.

### PREPARING PUPPY'S PLACE IN YOUR HOME

Researching your breed and finding a breeder are only two aspects of the "homework" you will have to do before bringing your Cocker puppy home. You will also have to prepare your home and family

for the new addition. Much as you would prepare a nursery for a newborn baby, you will need to designate a place in your home that will be the puppy's own. How you prepare your home will depend on how much freedom the dog will be allowed. Whatever you decide, you must ensure that he has a place that he can call his own.

When you bring your new puppy into your home, you are bringing him into what will become his home as well. Obviously, you did not buy a puppy so that he could take control of the home, but in order for a puppy to grow into a stable, well-adjusted dog, he has to feel comfortable in his surroundings. Remember, he is leaving the warmth and security of his mother and littermates, as well as the familiarity of the only place he has ever known, so it is important to make his transition as easy as possible. By preparing a place in your home for the puppy, you are making him feel as welcome as possible in a strange new place. It should not take him long to get used to it, but the sudden shock of being transplanted is somewhat traumatic for a young pup. Imagine how a small child would feel in the same situation—that is how your puppy must be feeling. It is up to you to reassure him and to let him know, "Little fellow, you are going to like it here!"

## WHAT YOU SHOULD BUY

### CRATE

To someone unfamiliar with the use of crates in dog training, it may seem like punishment to shut a dog in a crate, but this is not the case at all. More and more breeders and trainers recommend the crate as the preferred tool for pet puppies as well as show puppies. Crates are not cruel—crates have many humane and highly effective uses in dog care and training. For example, crate training is a popular and very successful housebreaking method. A crate can keep your dog safe during travel and, perhaps most importantly, a crate provides your dog with a place of his own in your home. It serves as a "doggie bedroom" of sorts—your Cocker Spaniel can curl up in his crate when he wants to sleep or when he just needs a break. Many dogs sleep in their crates overnight.

Top breeders around the world are convinced that crate training is the best way to housebreak and train a dog. Your pet shop will offer crates in a wide variety of sizes, styles and colors.

PHOTO COURTESY OF DOSKOCIL.

### PUPPY PROBLEMS
The majority of problems that are commonly seen in young pups will disappear as your dog gets older. However, how you deal with problems when he is young will determine how he reacts to discipline as an adult dog. It is important to establish who is boss (hopefully it will be you!) right away when you are first bonding with your dog. This bond will set the tone for the rest of your life together.

With soft bedding and a favorite toy inside, a crate becomes a cozy pseudo-den for your dog. Like his ancestors, he too will seek out the comfort and retreat of a den—you just happen to be providing him with something a little more luxurious than what his early ancestors enjoyed.

As far as purchasing a crate, the type that you buy is up to you. It will most likely be one of the two most popular types: wire or fiberglass. There are advantages and disadvantages to each type.

The wire crate is popular for use in the home, as it safely confines a dog while allowing him to feel part of his surroundings.

For example, a wire crate is more open, allowing the air to flow through and affording the dog a view of what is going on around him, while a fiberglass crate is sturdier. Both can double as travel crates, providing protection for the dog in the car. The size of the crate is another thing to consider. Puppies do not stay puppies forever—in fact, sometimes it seems as if they grow right before your eyes. A small crate may be fine for a young Cocker Spaniel pup, but it will not do him much good for long! Unless you have the money and the inclination to buy a new crate every time your pup has a growth spurt, it is better to get one that will accommodate your dog both as a pup and at full size. A medium-size crate will be necessary for a fully grown Cocker Spaniel, who stands approximately 14–15 inches high.

### BEDDING

A soft crate pad will help the dog feel more at home in his crate, and you may also like to give him a small blanket. These will take the place of the leaves, twigs, etc., that the pup would use in the wild to make a den; the pup can make his own "burrow" in the crate. Although your pup is far removed from his den-making ancestors, the denning instinct is still a part of his genetic makeup. Second, until you bring your pup home, he has been sleeping amid the warmth of his mother and littermates, and while a blanket is not the same as a warm, breathing body, it still

## CRATE-TRAINING TIPS

During crate training, you should partition off the section of the crate in which the pup stays. If he is given too big an area, this will hinder your training efforts. Crate training is based on the fact that a dog does not like to soil his sleeping quarters, so it is ineffective to keep a pup in an area that is so big that he can eliminate in one end and get far enough away from it to sleep. Also, you want to make the crate den-like for the pup. Blankets and a favorite toy will make the crate cozy for the small pup; as he grows, you may want to evict some of his "roommates" to make more room. It will take some coaxing at first, but be patient. Given some time to get used to it, your pup will adapt to his new home-within-a-home quite nicely.

provides heat and something with which to snuggle. You will want to wash your pup's bedding frequently in case he has an accident in his crate, and replace or remove any blanket or bedding that becomes ragged and starts to fall apart.

## Toys

Toys are a must for dogs of all ages, especially for curious, playful pups. Puppies are the "children" of the dog world, and what child does not love toys? Chew toys provide enjoyment to both dog and owner—your dog will enjoy playing with his favorite toys, while you will enjoy the fact that they distract him from your expensive shoes and leather sofa. Puppies love to chew; in fact, chewing is a physical need for pups as they are teething, and everything looks appetizing! The full range of your possessions—from old dish rag to Oriental rug—are fair game in the eyes of a teething pup. Puppies are not all that discerning when it comes to finding something literally to "sink their teeth into"—everything tastes great!

Cocker Spaniel puppies are fairly aggressive chewers and only the strongest, most durable toys should be offered to them. Breeders advise owners to be careful with stuffed toys, because they can become de-stuffed in no time. The overly excited pup may ingest the stuffing, which is neither nutritious nor digestible.

Similarly, squeaky toys are quite popular, but must be avoided for the Cocker. Perhaps a squeaky toy can be used as an aid in training, but not for free play. If a pup "disembowels" one of these, the small plastic squeaker inside can be dangerous if swallowed. Monitor the condition of all your pup's toys carefully and get rid of any that have been chewed to the point of becoming potentially dangerous.

Be careful of natural bones, which have a tendency to splinter into sharp, dangerous pieces. Also be careful of rawhide, which can turn into pieces that are easy to swallow and become a mushy mess on your carpet.

## Leash

A nylon leash is probably the best option, as it is the most resistant to puppy teeth should your pup take a liking to chewing on his leash. Of course, this is a habit that should be nipped in the bud,

**When you bring your Cocker puppy into your home, you must be prepared. Among the items to have on hand are safe toys, chew bones and a dog bed.**

but, if your pup likes to chew on his leash, he has a very slim chance of being able to chew through the strong nylon. Nylon leashes are also lightweight, which is good for a young Cocker puppy who is just getting used to the idea of walking on a leash. For everyday walking and safety purposes, the nylon leash is a good choice.

As your pup grows up and gets used to walking on the leash, and can do it politely, you may want to purchase a flexible leash. These leashes allow you to extend the length to give the dog a broader area to explore or to shorten the length to keep the dog close to you.

### COLLAR

Your pup should get used to wearing a collar all the time since you will want to attach his ID tags to it. Plus, you have to attach the leash to something! A lightweight nylon collar is a good choice; make sure that it fits snugly enough so that the pup cannot wriggle out of it, but is loose enough so that it will not be uncomfortably tight around the pup's neck. You should be able to fit a finger between the pup and the collar. It may take some time for your pup to get used to wearing the collar, but soon he will not even notice that it is there. Choke collars are made for training, but are not appropriate for

Most trainers recommend using a lightweight nylon leash for your Cocker Spaniel. Pet shops offer dozens of choices for collars and leashes, in different styles, colors and lengths.

**TRAINING TIP**

Training your puppy takes much patience and can be frustrating at times, but you should see results from your efforts. If you have a puppy that seems untrainable, take him to a trainer or behaviorist. The dog may have a personality problem that requires the help of a professional, or perhaps you need help in learning how to train your dog.

use on the Cocker as they can pull and badly damage the coat around the dog's neck.

### FOOD AND WATER BOWLS

Your pup will need two bowls, one for food and one for water. You may want two sets of bowls, one for inside and one for outside, depending on where the dog will be fed and where he will be spending time. Stainless steel or sturdy plastic bowls are popular choices. Plastic bowls are more chewable, but dogs tend not to chew on the steel variety, which can be sterilized. It is important to buy sturdy bowls since anything is in danger of being chewed by puppy teeth and you do not want your dog to be constantly chewing apart his bowl (for his safety and for your wallet!).

When shopping for bowls for your Cocker, seek out the special bowls designed to keep the dog's

Provide your Cocker Spaniel with durable food and water bowls. These bowls can be constructed of sturdy plastic, ceramic, clay or stainless steel.

# CHOOSE THE RIGHT COLLAR

**Buckle Collar**

The BUCKLE COLLAR is the standard collar used for everyday purpose. Be sure that you adjust the buckle on growing puppies. Check it every day. It can become too tight overnight! These collars can be made of leather or nylon. Attach your dog's identification tags to this collar.

**Choke Collar**

The CHOKE COLLAR is designed for training. It is constructed of highly polished steel so that it slides easily through the stainless steel loop. The idea is that the dog controls the pressure around his neck and he will stop pulling if the collar becomes uncomfortable. It is *not* suitable for use with the Cocker Spaniel.

**Halter**

The HALTER is for a trained dog that has to be restrained to prevent running away, chasing a cat and the like. Considered the most humane of all collars, it is frequently used on smaller dogs on which collars are not comfortable.

ears out of his food and water. Owners are always frustrated by having to clean the Cocker's long ears after every meal, snack and drink!

### CLEANING SUPPLIES
Until a pup is housebroken, you will be doing a lot of cleaning. "Accidents" will occur, which is okay in the beginning because the puppy does not know any better. All you can do is be prepared to clean up any accidents. Old rags, paper towels, newspapers and a safe disinfectant are good to have on hand.

### BEYOND THE BASICS
The items previously discussed are the bare necessities. You will find out what else you need as

## NATURAL TOXINS
Examine your grass and landscaping before bringing your puppy home. Many varieties of plants have leaves, stems or flowers that are toxic if ingested, and you can depend on a curious puppy to investigate them. Ask your vet for information on poisonous plants or research them at your library.

   If you see your dog carrying a piece of vegetation in his mouth, approach him in a quiet, disinterested manner, avoid eye contact, pet him and gradually remove the plant from his mouth. Alternatively, offer him a treat and maybe he'll drop the plant on his own accord. Be sure no toxic plants are growing in your own yard or kept in your home.

Responsible, law-abiding dog owners pick up their dogs' dropping whenever they are in public. Pooper-scooper devices make the job quick and easy.

you go along—grooming supplies, flea/tick protection, baby gates to partition a room, etc. These things will vary depending on your situation, but it is important that you have everything you need to feed and make your Cocker Spaniel comfortable in his first few days at home.

**PUPPY-PROOFING YOUR HOME**
Aside from making sure that your Cocker Spaniel will be comfortable in your home, you also have to make sure that your home is safe for your Cocker Spaniel. This means taking precautions that your pup will not get into anything he should not get into and that there is nothing within his reach that may harm him should he sniff it, chew it, inspect it, etc. This probably seems obvious since, while you are primarily concerned with your pup's safety, at the same time you do not want your belongings to be ruined.

Breakables should be placed out of reach if your dog is to have full run of the house. If he is to be limited to certain places within the house, keep any potentially dangerous items in the "off-limits" areas. An electrical cord can pose a danger should the puppy decide to taste it—and who is going to convince a pup that it would not make a great chew toy? Cords should be fastened tightly against the wall, out of puppy's sight and away

from his teeth! If your dog is going to spend time in a crate, make sure that there is nothing near his crate that he can reach if he sticks his curious little nose or paws through the openings. Just as you would with a child, keep all household cleaners and chemicals where the pup cannot get to them.

It is also important to make sure that the outside of your home is safe. Of course your puppy should never be unsupervised, but a pup let loose in the

yard will want to run and explore, and he should be granted that freedom. Do not let a fence give you a false sense of security; you would be surprised how crafty (and persistent) a dog can be in figuring out how to dig under and squeeze his way through small holes, or to jump or climb over a fence. The remedy is to make the fence high enough so that it really is impossible for your dog to get over it (about 5 feet should suffice), and well embedded into the ground. Be

## HOW VACCINES WORK

If you've just bought a puppy, you surely know the importance of having your pup vaccinated, but do you understand how vaccines work? Vaccines contain the same bacteria or viruses that cause the disease you want to prevent, but they have been chemically modified so that they don't cause any harm. Instead, the vaccine causes your dog to produce antibodies that fight the harmful bacteria. Thus, if your dog is exposed to the disease in the future, the antibodies will destroy the viruses or bacteria.

sure to secure any gaps in the fence and check the fence periodically so that you can make repairs as needed. A very determined pup may return to the same spot to "work on it" until he is able to get through.

## FIRST TRIP TO THE VET

You have picked out your puppy, and your home and family are ready. Now all you have to do is collect your Cocker Spaniel from the breeder and the fun begins, right? Well...not so fast. Something else you need to prepare is your pup's first trip to the veterinarian. Perhaps the breeder can recommend someone in the area that specializes in Cockers, or maybe you know some other Cocker Spaniel owners who can

Make your new Cocker Spaniel puppy feel at home, but be certain that everything breakable and chewable is kept out of jaws' way. Give the pup suitable chew toys to occupy his growing teeth.

suggest a good vet. Either way, you should have an appointment arranged for your pup before you pick him up and plan on taking him for an examination before bringing him home.

The pup's first visit will consist of an overall examination to make sure that the pup does not have any problems that are not apparent to you. The veterinarian will also set up a schedule for the pup's vaccinations; the breeder will inform you of which ones the pup has already received and the vet can continue from there.

Select a skilled vet close to your home and have your Cocker examined on a schedule recommended by the vet.

## PET INSURANCE

Just like you can insure your car, your house and your own health, you likewise can insure your dog's health. Investigate a pet insurance policy by talking to your vet. Depending on the age of your dog, the breed and the kind of coverage you desire, your policy can be very affordable. Most policies cover accidental injuries, poisoning and thousands of medical problems and illnesses, including cancers. Some carriers also offer routine care and immunization coverage.

## INTRODUCTION TO THE FAMILY

Everyone in the house will be excited about the puppy's coming home and will want to pet him and play with him, but it is best to make the introductions low-key so as not to overwhelm the puppy. He is apprehensive already. It is the first time he has been separated from his mother and the breeder, and the ride to your home is likely the first time he has been in a car. The last thing you want to do is smother him, as this will only frighten him further. This is not to say that human contact is not extremely necessary at this stage, because this is the time when a connection between the pup and his human family is formed. Gentle petting and soothing words

should help console him, as well as just putting him down and letting him explore on his own (under your watchful eye, of course).

The pup may approach the family members or may busy himself with exploring for a while. Gradually, each person should spend some time with the pup, one at a time, crouching down to get as close to the pup's level as possible and letting him sniff their hands and petting him gently. He definitely needs human attention and he needs to be touched—this is how to form an immediate bond. Just remember that the pup is experiencing a lot of things for the first time, at the same time. There are new people, new noises, new smells and new things to investigate, so be gentle, be affectionate and be as comforting as you can be.

## YOUR PUP'S FIRST NIGHT HOME

You have traveled home with your new charge safely in his crate or on a passenger's lap. He's been to the vet for a thorough checkup; he's been weighed, his papers examined; perhaps he's even been vaccinated and wormed as well. He's met the family, including the excited children and the less-than-happy cat. He's explored his area, his new bed, the yard and anywhere else he's been permitted. He's eaten his first meal at home and relieved himself in the proper place. He's heard lots of new sounds, smelled new friends and seen more of the outside world than ever before. That was just

A Cocker Spaniel provides an endless supply of cuddles for his whole family.

Once accustomed to his home, the Cocker can make himself comfortable anywhere!

the first day! Your puppy is tired out and is ready for bed...or so you think!

It's puppy's first night and you are ready to say "Good night"—keep in mind that this is puppy's first night ever to be sleeping alone. His dam and littermates are no longer at paw's length and he's a bit scared, cold and lonely. Be reassuring to your new family member, but this is not the time to spoil him and give in to his inevitable whining.

Puppies whine. They whine to let others know where they are and hopefully to get company out of it. Place your pup in his new bed or crate in his room and close the crate door. Mercifully, he may fall asleep without a peep. When the inevitable occurs, ignore the whining; he is fine. Be strong and keep his interest in mind. Do not allow your heart to become guilty and visit the pup. He will fall asleep.

Many breeders recommend placing a piece of bedding from his former home in his new bed so that he recognizes the scent of his littermates. Others still advise placing a hot-water bottle in his bed for warmth. The latter may be a good idea provided the pup doesn't attempt to suckle—he'll get good and wet and may not fall asleep so fast.

Puppy's first night can be somewhat stressful for the pup and his new family. Remember that you are setting the tone of night-time at your house. Unless you want to play with your pup every night at 10 p.m., midnight and 2 a.m., don't initiate the habit. Your family will thank you, and soon so will your pup!

## PREVENTING PUPPY PROBLEMS

### SOCIALIZATION

Now that you have done all of the preparatory work and have helped your pup get accustomed to his new home and family, it is about time for

you to have some fun! Socializing your Cocker Spaniel pup gives you the opportunity to show off your new friend, and your pup gets to reap the benefits of being an adorable furry creature that people will want to pet and, in general, think is absolutely precious!

Besides getting to know his new family, your puppy should be exposed to other people, animals and situations, but of course he must not come into close contact with dogs you don't know well until his course of

**SKULL & CROSSBONES**

Thoroughly puppy-proof your house before bringing your puppy home. Never use cockroach or rodent poisons or plant fertilizers in any area accessible to the puppy. Avoid the use of toilet cleaners. Most dogs are born with "toilet-bowl sonar" and will take a drink if the lid is left open. Keep the trash secured and out of reach. Be especially careful of antifreeze, as dogs are attracted to its taste and only a small amount can kill a dog quickly.

injections is fully complete. Socialization will help him become well adjusted as he grows up and less prone to being timid or fearful of the new things he will encounter. Your pup's socialization began at the breeder's, but now it is your responsibility to continue it.

The socialization he receives up until the age of 12 weeks is the most critical, as this is the time when he forms his impressions of the outside world. Be especially careful during the eight-to-ten-week-old period, also known as the fear period. The interaction he receives during this time should be gentle and reassuring. Lack of socialization can manifest itself in fear and aggression as the dog grows up. He needs lots of human contact, affection, handling and

Children and Cockers can bond closely. A well-socialized puppy, exposed to lots of different people and circumstances, will grow up into a friendly, well-adjusted adult dog.

Cockers eagerly enjoy the company of his owners and other pets in the home. This happy bunch shows that the feeling is mutual.

exposure to other animals.

Once your pup has received his necessary vaccinations, feel free to take him out and about (on his leash, of course). Walk him around the neighborhood, take him on your daily errands, let people pet him, let him meet other dogs and pets, etc. Puppies do not have to try to make friends; there will be no shortage of people who will want to introduce themselves. Just make sure that you carefully supervise each meeting. If the neighborhood children want to say hello, for example, that is great—children and pups most often make great companions. However, sometimes an excited child can unintentionally handle a pup too roughly, or an overzealous pup can playfully nip a little too hard. You want to make socialization experiences positive ones. What a pup learns during this very formative stage will impact his attitude toward future encounters. You want your dog to be comfortable around everyone. A pup that has a bad

experience with a child may grow up to be a dog that is shy around or aggressive toward children.

### CONSISTENCY IN TRAINING

Dogs, being pack animals, naturally need a leader, or else they try to establish dominance in their packs. When you bring a dog into your family, the choice of who becomes the leader and who becomes the pack is entirely up to you! Your pup's intuitive quest for dominance, coupled with the fact that it is nearly impossible to look at an adorable Cocker pup with his "puppy-dog" eyes and not cave in, give the pup almost an unfair advantage in getting the upper hand!

A pup will definitely test the waters to see what he can and

### MANNERS MATTER
During the socialization process, a puppy should meet people, experience different environments and definitely be exposed to other canines. Through playing and interacting with other dogs, your puppy will learn lessons, ranging from controlling the pressure of his jaws by biting his littermates to the inner-workings of the canine pack that he will apply to his human relationships for the rest of his life. That is why removing a puppy from the litter too early (before eight weeks) can be detrimental to the pup's development.

cannot do. Do not give in to those pleading eyes—stand your ground when it comes to disciplining the pup and make sure that all family members do the same. It will only confuse the pup when Mother tells him to get off the couch when he is used to sitting up there with Father to watch the nightly news. Avoid discrepancies by having all members of the household decide on the rules before the pup even comes home…and be consistent in enforcing them! Early training shapes the dog's personality, so you cannot be unclear in what you expect.

## COMMON PUPPY PROBLEMS

The best way to prevent puppy problems is to be proactive in stopping an undesirable behavior as soon as it starts. The old saying "You can't teach an old dog new tricks" does not necessarily hold true, but it *is* true that it is much easier to discourage bad behavior in a young developing pup than to wait until the pup's bad behavior becomes the adult dog's bad habit. There are some problems that are especially prevalent in puppies as they develop.

### NIPPING

As puppies start to teethe, they feel the need to sink their teeth into anything available…unfortunately, that includes your fingers, arms, hair and toes. You may find

this behavior cute for about the first five seconds…until you feel just how sharp those puppy teeth are. This is something you want to discourage immediately and consistently with a firm "No!" (or whatever number of firm "Nos" it takes for him to understand that you mean business). Then replace your finger with an appropriate chew toy. While this behavior is merely annoying when the dog is young, it can become dangerous as your Cocker Spaniel's adult teeth grow in and his jaws develop, and he continues to think it is okay to gnaw on human appendages. Your Cocker does not mean any harm with a friendly nip, but he also does not know his own strength.

### CRYING/WHINING

Your pup will often cry, whine, whimper, howl or make some type of commotion when he is left alone. This is basically his way of

The Cocker's "puppy dog" eyes can render most new owners helpless, giving the pup an unfair advantage in getting his way! Be consistent and firm in your training or you will lose the "human advantage."

calling out for attention to make sure that you know he is there and that you have not forgotten about him. He feels insecure when he is left alone, when you are out of the house and he is in his crate or when you are in another part of the house and he

cannot see you. The noise he is making is an expression of the anxiety he feels at being alone, so he needs to be taught that being alone is okay. You are not actually training the dog to stop making noise, you are training him to feel comfortable when he is alone and thus removing the need for him to make the noise. This is where the crate with cozy bedding and a toy comes in handy. You want to know that he is safe when you are not there to supervise, and you know that he will be safe in his crate rather than roaming freely about the house. In order for the pup to stay in his crate without making a fuss, he needs to be comfortable in his crate. On that note, it is extremely important that the crate is never used as a form of punishment, or the pup will develop a negative association with the crate.

Accustom the pup to the crate in short, gradually increasing time intervals in which you put him in the crate, maybe with a treat, and stay in the room with him. If he cries or makes a fuss, do not go to him, but stay in his sight. Gradually he will realize that staying in his crate is all right without your help, and it will not be so traumatic for him when you are not around. You may want to leave the radio on softly when you leave the house; the sound of human voices may be comforting to him.

### CHEWING TIPS

Chewing goes hand in hand with nipping in the sense that a teething puppy is always looking for a way to soothe his aching gums. In this case, instead of chewing on you, he may have taken a liking to your favorite shoe or something else that he should not be chewing. Again, realize that this is a normal canine behavior that does not need to be discouraged, only redirected. Your pup just needs to be taught what is acceptable to chew on and what is off-limits. Consistently tell him "No!" when you catch him chewing on something forbidden and give him a chew toy.

Conversely, praise him when you catch him chewing on something appropriate. In this way, you are discouraging the inappropriate behavior and reinforcing the desired behavior. The puppy's chewing should stop after his adult teeth have come in, but an adult dog continues to chew for various reasons—perhaps because he is bored, needs to relieve tension or just likes to chew. That is why it is important to redirect his chewing when he is still young.

Your puppy looks up to you, his new pack leader, to provide him with all that he needs—not the least of which is plenty of love and affection!

# COCKER SPANIEL

## DIETARY AND FEEDING CONSIDERATIONS

Today the choices of food for your Cocker Spaniel are many and varied. There are simply dozens of brands of food in all sorts of flavors and textures, ranging from puppy diets to those for seniors. There are even hypoallergenic and low-calorie diets available. Because your Cocker's food has a bearing on coat, health and temperament, it is essential that the most suitable diet is selected for a Cocker Spaniel of his age. It is fair to say, however, that even dedicated owners can be somewhat perplexed by the enormous range of foods available. Only understanding what is best for your dog will help you reach an informed decision.

Dog foods are produced in three basic types: dry, semi-moist and canned. Dry foods are useful for the cost-conscious, for overall they tend to be less expensive than semi-moist or canned. Dry foods contain the least fat and the most preservatives. In general, canned foods are made up of 60–70% water, while semi-moist ones often contain so much sugar that they are perhaps the least preferred by owners, even though their dogs seem to like them.

When selecting your dog's diet, three stages of development must be considered: the puppy stage, the adult stage and the senior stage.

### PUPPY STAGE

Puppies instinctively want to suck milk from their mother's teats and a normal puppy will exhibit this behavior from just a few moments following birth. If puppies do not attempt to suckle within the first half-hour or so, the breeder should encourage them to do so by placing them on the nipples, having selected ones with plenty of milk. This early milk supply is important in providing colostrum to protect

### SELDOM FINICKY

The Cocker Spaniel is seldom a finicky eater. In fact, owners are cautioned not to allow their dogs to overeat and become too heavy early on or obesity can develop in maturity.

the puppies during the first eight to ten weeks of their lives. Although a mother's milk is much better than any milk formula, despite there being some excellent ones available, if the puppies do not feed, the breeder will have to hand-feed them. For those with less experience, advice from a veterinarian is important so that not only the right quantity of milk is fed but also that of correct quality, fed at suitably frequent intervals, usually every two hours during the first few days of life.

Your breeder should recommend the diet for Cockers with which she has had success. A balanced diet is required in order to keep the Cocker fit and healthy.

## FEEDING TIPS

Dog food must be served at room temperature, neither too hot nor too cold. Fresh water, changed often and served in a clean bowl, is mandatory, especially when feeding dry food.

Never feed your dog from the table while you are eating, and never feed your dog leftovers from your own meal. They usually contain too much fat and too much seasoning.

Dogs must chew their food. Hard pellets are excellent; soups and stews are to be avoided.

Don't add leftovers or any extras to commercial dog food. The normal food is usually balanced, and adding something extra destroys the balance.

Except for age-related changes, dogs do not require dietary variations. They can be fed the same diet, day after day, without their becoming bored or ill.

Puppies should be allowed to nurse from their mothers for about the first six weeks, although from the third or fourth week the breeder will begin to introduce small portions of suitable solid food. Most breeders like to introduce alternate milk and meat meals initially, building up to weaning time.

By the time the puppies are seven or a maximum of eight weeks old, they should be fully weaned and fed solely on a proprietary puppy food. Selection of the most suitable, good-quality diet at this time is essential, for a puppy's fastest growth rate is during the first year of life. Veterinarians and breeders

## FOOD PREFERENCE

Selecting the best dry dog food is difficult. There is no majority consensus among veterinary scientists as to the value of nutrient analysis (protein, fat, fiber, moisture, ash, cholesterol, minerals, etc.). All agree that feeding trials are what matter most, but you also have to consider the individual dog. The dog's weight, age and activity level, and what pleases his taste, all must be considered. It is probably best to take the advice of your veterinarian. Every dog's dietary requirements vary, even during the lifetime of a particular dog.

If your dog is fed a good dry food, he does not require supplements of meat or vegetables. Dogs do appreciate a little variety in their diets, so you may choose to stay with the same brand but vary the flavor. Alternatively, you may wish to add a little flavored stock to give a difference to the taste.

are usually able to offer advice in this regard. The frequency of meals will be reduced over time, and when a young Cocker Spaniel has reached the age of about one year old, he can be switched to an adult diet.

Puppy and junior diets should be well balanced for the needs of your dog so that, except in certain circumstances, additional vitamins, minerals and proteins will not be required.

### ADULT DIETS

A dog is considered an adult when it has stopped growing, so in general the Cocker's diet can be changed to an adult one around the one-year mark, usually at about 10 to 12 months of age. Again you should rely upon your veterinarian or breeder to recommend an acceptable maintenance diet. Major dog food manufacturers specialize in this type of food, and it is just necessary for you to select the one best suited to your dog's needs. Active dogs may have different requirements than sedate dogs.

### SENIOR DIETS

As dogs get older, their metabolism changes. The older dog usually exercises less, moves more slowly and sleeps more. This change in lifestyle and physiological performance requires a change in diet. Since

# A Worthy Investment

Veterinary studies have proven that a balanced high-quality diet pays off in your dog's coat quality, behavior and activity level. Invest in premium brands for the maximum payoff with your dog.

these changes take place slowly, they might not be recognizable. What is easily recognizable is weight gain. By continuing to feed your dog an adult-maintenance diet when he is slowing down metabolically, your dog will gain weight. Obesity in an older dog compounds the health problems that already accompany old age.

As your dog gets older, few of his organs function up to par. The kidneys slow down and the intestines become less efficient. These age-related factors are best handled with a change in diet and a change in feeding schedule to give smaller portions that are more easily digested.

There is no single best diet for every older dog. While many dogs do well on light or senior diets, other dogs do better on puppy diets or other special premium diets such as lamb and rice. Be sensitive to your senior Cocker Spaniel's diet and this will help control other problems that may arise with your old friend.

## WATER

Just as your dog needs proper nutrition from his food, water is an essential "nutrient" as well. Water keeps the dog's body properly hydrated and promotes normal function of the body's systems. During housebreaking, it is necessary to keep an eye on how much water your Cocker Spaniel is drinking, but, once he is reliably trained, he should have access to clean fresh water at all times. Make sure that the dog's water bowl is clean, and change the water often, making sure that water is always available for your dog, especially if you feed dry food.

## EXERCISE

By birth, the Cocker Spaniel is a hunting dog, which translates to "I need plenty of exercise to stay sane!" Although the Cocker doesn't need as much constant exercise as some of the other sporting breeds, he does need lots of activity and exercise. A sedentary lifestyle is as harmful to a dog as it is to a person. The Cocker is a fairly active breed

### GRAIN-BASED DIETS

Some less expensive dog foods are based on grains and other plant proteins. While these products may appear to be attractively priced, many breeders prefer a diet based on animal proteins and believe that they are more conducive to your dog's health. Many grain-based diets rely on soy protein, which may cause flatulence (passing gas).

There are many cases, however, when your dog might require a special diet. These special requirements should only be recommended by your veterinarian.

that enjoys exercise, but you don't have to be an Olympic athlete to provide your dog with the activity he needs! Regular walks, play sessions in the fenced yard or letting the dog run free in a fenced enclosure under your supervision are sufficient forms of exercise for the Cocker. For those who are more ambitious, you will find that your Cocker Spaniel also enjoys long walks, an occasional hike or even a swim!

If not given ample opportu-

Water is an absolute must. It should be fresh, clean and suitable for drinking by a human.

nity to exercise, the Cocker may become quite obese, which can be very detrimental to the dog's health. Bear in mind that an overweight dog should never be suddenly over-exercised; instead, he should be allowed to increase exercise slowly. Also keep in mind that exercise is not only essential to keeping the dog's body fit, it is essential to his mental well-being. A bored dog will find something to do, which often manifests itself in some type of destructive behavior. In this sense, it is just as essential for the owner's mental well-being!

## GROOMING

### GENERAL COAT CARE
Much of what initially attracts people to the Cocker Spaniel is the breed's wide array of colors and beautiful long coat. We wish we could tell you that it does not take much to maintain that look.

---

### "DOES THIS COLLAR MAKE ME LOOK FAT?"
While humans may obsess about how they look and how trim their bodies are, many people believe that extra weight on their dogs is a good thing. The truth is, pets should not be over- or under-weight, as both can lead to or signal sickness. In order to tell how fit your pet is, run your hands over his ribs. Are his ribs buried under a layer of fat or are they sticking out considerably? If your pet is within his normal weight range, you should be able to feel the ribs easily, but they should not protrude abnormally. If you stand above him, the outline of his body should resemble an hourglass. Some breeds do tend to be leaner while some are a bit stockier, but making sure your dog is the right weight for his breed will certainly contribute to his good health.

The show Cocker will require the assistance of a professional groomer. To keep your Cocker in a pet clip, less maintenance is required.

that are so prevalent today.

The Cocker Spaniel does shed, but regular grooming not only keeps that shed hair from floating about your home but also promotes healthy skin. Frequent grooming also gives you an opportunity to catch any burgeoning health problems. Notice should always be taken of any changes in skin, coat, ears and eyes, and those changes should be discussed with your veterinarian.

### GROOMING THE PUPPY

Undoubtedly the breeder from whom you purchased your Cocker will have begun to accus-

Unfortunately, we can't. Your Cocker will only have that special show-dog look with expertise and diligence—usually far more expertise and diligence than the average pet owner is willing to invest. This does not mean that a Cocker Spaniel's coat must be a full-time chore. The short pet trims are attractive and as easy to manage as any reasonably coated breed.

The amount of grooming required is dependent upon how the coat is kept and how the owner likes the dog to look. Coat texture is a major consideration if the owner would like to keep the coat long; the proper silky, straight coat texture required in the breed standard is easier to maintain than the cottony coats

## GROOMING EQUIPMENT

How much equipment you purchase will depend on how much grooming you will do yourself. Here's a checklist of the basics:

- Pin brush
- Grooming table
- Slicker brush
- Metal comb
- Scissors
- Electric clippers
- Rubber mat
- Dog shampoo
- Spray hose attachment
- Blow dryer
- Towels
- Ear cleaner
- Cotton wipes
- Nail clippers

tom the puppy to grooming just as soon as there was enough hair to brush. You must continue on with grooming sessions or begin them at once if for some reason they have not been started. You and your Cocker Spaniel will spend considerable time over the months and years involved with this activity, so it is imperative that you both learn to cooperate in the endeavor to make it an easy and pleasant experience.

Do not attempt to groom your puppy on the floor. The puppy will attempt to get away from you when he has decided that enough is enough, and you will spend a good part of your time chasing the puppy around the room. Plus, sitting on the floor for long stretches of time is not the most comfortable position in the world for the average adult.

The Cocker Spaniel puppy should be taught to lie on his side to be groomed. As your Cocker Spaniel grows and develops a heavier adult coat, you will find the bit of effort you invested in teaching the puppy to lie on his side will be time well spent, as the puppy will be kept in that position for most of the brushing process. Your Cocker Spaniel will also have to be kept in the standing position for some of his grooming, but the lying position is a bit more difficult for the puppy to learn.

Begin this training by laying

Regular grooming is necessary. It keeps your Cocker looking well and it keeps shedding to a minimum.

the puppy down on his side on the table. Pick the puppy up as you would a lamb, hold him to your chest and lean down with the puppy until he is resting on the table. Speak reassuringly to the puppy, stroking his head and rump. (This is a good time to practice the "stay" command.) Do this a number of times before you attempt to do any grooming. Repeat the process until your puppy understands what he is

The time you spend accustoming your pup to being groomed will pay off throughout your Cocker's life.

Although the show coat is time-consuming and more costly to maintain, the end results are glorious and rewarding.

supposed to do when you place him on the grooming table.

### EQUIPMENT

The first piece of equipment that you should obtain is a grooming table. A grooming table can be purchased at your local pet-supply store. An unsteady table is a very frightening thing for any dog and you will be wasting time and energy if you do not purchase a suitable sturdy table on which to groom your Cocker. Make sure that whatever kind of table you use is of a height at which you can work comfortably. Adjustable-height grooming tables are available at most pet shops.

Show Cockers are among the most patient creatures on earth. Preparing the coat for exhibition requires hours of bathing, brushing, trimming and primping.

You will also need to invest in two brushes, a steel comb with medium and fine teeth, barber's scissors and nail clippers. Unless you keep your dog's

coat extremely short, a blow dryer with heat control is a must for after the bath. Electric clippers can be very useful as well when your Cocker has developed his adult coat. Consider the fact that you will be using these grooming tools for many years to come, so buy the best of these items that you can afford.

The brushes that you will need are a pin brush, sometimes called a "Poodle brush," and a "slicker brush." All of these supplies can be purchased at your local pet shop or at any dog show.

### GROOMING THE ADULT COCKER

Ideally you and your Cocker have spent the many months between puppyhood and full maturity learning to assist each other through the grooming process. The two of you have survived the changing of the puppy coat and the arrival of the entirely differ-

ent adult hair. The hair of the adult Cocker is more profuse and, if allowed to grow unchecked, will become very long.

While one might expect grooming an adult Cocker to be a

A suitable grooming table with an arm is necessary for properly grooming the Cocker. A grooming table saves you time and physical exertion.

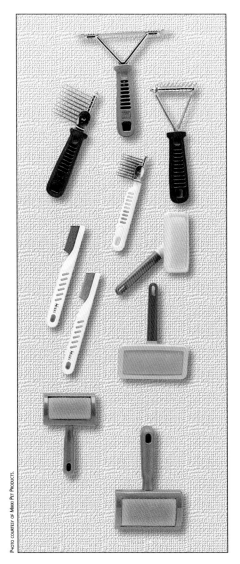

monumental task, this is not necessarily so. The important thing is consistency. A few minutes a day, every day, precludes your dog's hair becoming a tangled mess, which may take you hours to undo. By now, though, the two of you have been practicing the brushing routine for so long that it has undoubtedly become second nature to both of you.

Some owners find the long flowing coat particularly attractive and wish to keep it that way at all times. This, of course, is an absolute necessity if the dog is to be shown. Maintaining a show coat is not for the complete novice and we strongly suggest that you consult the breeder from whom you purchased your Cocker or a professional groomer for help with the show coat.

One very important thing to remember—no Cocker should

Your local pet shop should carry a complete line of grooming tools from which you can select those most suitable for grooming your Cocker.

PHOTO COURTESY OF MIKKI PET PRODUCTS.

These show Cockers await their opportunity to show off their glamorous coats in the show ring.

Most pet owners find maintaining the long coat is an extremely demanding task and use scissors to cut the coat back to a manageable length. Electric clippers can be used to remove the hair from the frequently matted "armpits" (under the legs where they join the body) and under the dog's stomach. The coat on the head, neck and body is also trimmed very short, leaving the hair on the ears longer. The hair on the ears and legs is left longer to maintain the distinctive Cocker look. Hair should be removed from between the toe pads. You can use barber scissors or electric clippers to accomplish this.

ever be bathed until each and every mat and tangle is worked out from the coat. If you bathe a matted dog, the hair will "felt" and become a solid mass that will have to be cut out down to the skin. This will not only put an ugly hole in the middle of your dog's furnishings, it could be extremely risky as you attempt to avoid damaging the skin.

The Cocker has a lot of hair! An electric clipper is required to trim down the long coat for the pet clip.

### BATHING

Dogs do not need to be bathed as often as humans, but regular bathing is essential for healthy skin and a healthy, shiny coat. Again, like most anything, if you accustom your pup to being bathed as a puppy, it will be second nature by the time he grows up. You want your dog to be at ease in the bath or else it could end up a wet, soapy, messy ordeal for both of you!

Brush your Cocker Spaniel thoroughly before wetting his coat. This will get rid of most mats and tangles, which are harder to remove when the coat is wet. Make sure that your dog has a good non-slip surface to

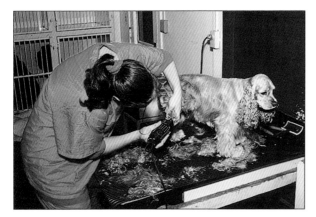

Once the dog has been thoroughly shampooed, he requires an equally thorough rinsing. Shampoo left in the coat can be irritating to the skin. Protect his eyes from the shampoo by shielding them with your hand and directing the flow of water in the opposite direction. You should also avoid getting water

stand on. Begin by wetting the dog's coat. A shower or hose attachment is necessary for thoroughly wetting and rinsing the coat. Check the water temperature to make sure that it is neither too hot nor too cold.

Next, apply shampoo to the dog's coat and work it into a good lather. You should purchase a shampoo that is made for dogs. Do not use a product made for human hair. Wash the head last; you do not want shampoo to drip into the dog's eyes while you are washing the rest of his body. Work the shampoo all the way down to the skin. You can use this opportunity to check the skin for any bumps, bites or other abnormalities. Do not neglect any area of the body—get all of the hard-to-reach places.

## BATHING BEAUTY

The use of human soap products like shampoo, bubble bath and hand soap can be damaging to a dog's coat and skin. Human products are too strong; they remove the protective oils coating the dog's hair and skin that make him water-resistant. Use only shampoo made especially for dogs. You may like to use a medicated shampoo, which will help to keep external parasites at bay.

Once you are sure that the dog is thoroughly rinsed, squeeze the excess water out of his coat with your hand and dry him with a heavy towel. Then finish the job with a blow dryer on a low heat setting, brushing as you dry. In cold weather, never allow your dog outside with a wet coat.

There are "dry bath" products on the market, which are sprays and powders intended for spot cleaning, that can be used between regular baths if necessary. They are not substitutes for regular baths, but they are easy to use for touch-ups as they do not require rinsing.

If you brush your Cocker every day, his coat will be shiny, clean and full.

The Cocker's long coat can pick up debris from the outdoors, so be sure to check the coat thoroughly after time spent outside.

his ears frequently, this usually indicates a problem. If his ears have an unusual odor, this is a sure sign of mite infestation or infection, and a signal to have his ears checked by the veterinarian.

### NAIL CLIPPING
Your Cocker should be accustomed to having his nails trimmed at an early age, since it will be part of your maintenance routine throughout his life. Not only does it look nicer, but long nails can be sharp and scratch someone unintentionally. Also, a long nail has a better chance of ripping and bleeding, or of causing the feet to spread. A good rule of thumb is that if you can hear your dog's nails' clicking on the floor when he walks, his

in the ear canal. Be prepared for your dog to shake out his coat— you might want to stand back, but make sure you have a hold on the dog to keep him from running through the house.

### EAR CLEANING
The ears should be kept clean and any excess hair inside the ears should be carefully plucked out. Ears can be cleaned with cotton balls or wipes and an ear-cleaning product made for dogs. Be on the lookout for any signs of infection or ear-mite infestation. If your Cocker has been shaking his head or scratching at

nails are too long.

Before you start cutting, make sure you can identify the "quick" in each nail. The quick is a blood vessel that runs through the center of each nail and grows rather close to the end. It will bleed if accidentally cut, which will be quite painful for the dog as it contains nerve endings. Keep some type of clotting agent on hand, such as a styptic pencil or styptic powder (the type used for shaving). This will stop the bleeding quickly when applied to the end of the cut nail. Do not panic if this happens, just stop the bleeding and talk soothingly to your dog. Once he has calmed down, move on to the next nail. It is better to clip a little at a time, particularly with black-nailed dogs.

Hold your pup steady as you begin trimming his nails; you do not want him to make any sudden movements or run away. Talk to him soothingly and stroke him as you clip. Holding his foot in your hand, simply

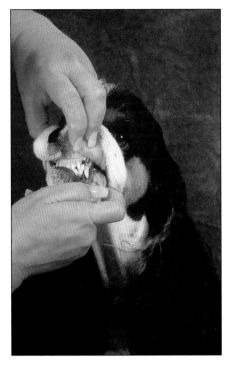

Make dental care part of your Cocker's grooming routine. Weekly brushing with canine tooth-care products will keep your dog's teeth and gums clean and healthy.

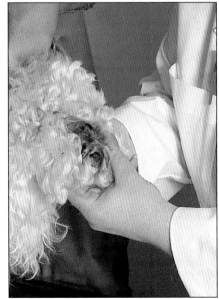

The hair on the bottom of the feet must be trimmed to prevent excess hair from matting and causing discomfort to the dog.

## NAIL FILING

You can purchase an electric tool to grind down a dog's nails rather than cut them. Some dogs don't seem to mind the electric grinder but will object strongly to nail clippers. Your dog's reactions to his pedicures will help you make the right choice.

## Nail Clipping

Quick

Cut Line

Nail Casing

**DARK-COLORED NAIL**

With black or dark nails, it's best to clip only a small bit of the nail at a time or to use a file where the quick is not visible.

**LIGHT-COLORED NAIL**

In light-colored nails, clipping is much simpler because you can see the vein (or quick) that grows inside the casing.

take off the end of each nail in one quick clip. You can purchase nail clippers that are specially made for dogs; you can probably find them wherever you buy pet or grooming supplies.

## TRAVELING WITH YOUR DOG

### CAR TRAVEL

You should accustom your Cocker Spaniel to riding in a car at an early age. You may or may not take him in the car often, but at the very least he will need to go to the vet and you do not want these trips to be traumatic for the dog or a big hassle for you. The safest way for a dog to ride in the car is in his crate. If he uses a crate in the house, you can use the same crate for travel.

Put the pup in the crate and see how he reacts. If he seems uneasy, you can have a passenger hold him on his lap while you drive. Another option is a specially made safety harness for dogs, which straps the dog in much like a seat belt. Do not let the dog roam loose in the vehicle—this is very dangerous! If you should stop short, your dog can be thrown and injured. If the dog starts climbing on you and pestering you while you are driving, you will not be able to concentrate on the road. It is an unsafe situation for everyone— human and canine.

For long trips, be prepared to stop to let the dog relieve himself. Bring along whatever you need to clean up after him. You should take along some paper towels and perhaps some old rags for use should he have a potty accident in the car or suffer from motion sickness.

### AIR TRAVEL

Contact your chosen airline before proceeding with travel plans that include your Cocker Spaniel. The dog will be required to travel in a fiberglass crate and you should always check in advance with the airline regarding specific requirements for the crate's size, type and labeling. Also check with the airline's restrictions on transporting pets, as many do not do this during the summer months.

To help put the dog at ease, be sure that he is well accus-

**TRAVEL ALERT**

When you travel with your dog, it's a good idea to take along water from home or to buy bottled water for the trip. In areas where water is sometimes chemically treated and sometimes comes right out of the ground, you can prevent adverse reactions to this essential part of your dog's diet.

**TRAVEL TIP**

Never leave your dog alone in the car. In hot weather, your dog can die from the high temperature inside a closed vehicle; even a car parked in the shade can heat up very quickly. Leaving the window open is dangerous as well since the dog can hurt himself trying to get out.

*Cockers can be safely secured in the car with a safety harness attached to the seat belt.*

tomed to the crate in which he will be traveling, and give him one of his favorite toys in the crate. Do not feed the dog for several hours prior to checking in so that you minimize his need to relieve himself. Some airlines require you to provide documentation as to when the dog has last been fed. In any case, a light meal is best. For long trips, you will have to attach bowls for food and water, and a portion of food, to the outside of the dog's

crate so that airline employees can tend to your Cocker between legs of the trip.

Make sure that your dog is properly identified and that your contact information appears on his ID tags and on his crate. Your Cocker Spaniel will travel in a different area of the plane than the human passengers, so every rule must be strictly followed to prevent the risk of getting separated from your dog. Transporting animals is rather routine for large carriers, but you always want to play it safe.

VACATIONS AND BOARDING

So you want to take a family vacation—and you want to include *all* members of the family. You would probably make arrangements for accommodations ahead of time anyway, but this is especially important when traveling with a dog. You do not want to make an

overnight stop at the only place around for miles and find out that they do not allow dogs. Also, you do not want to reserve a place for your family without confirming that you are traveling with a dog because, if it is against the hotel's policy, you may not have a place to stay.

Alternatively, if you are traveling and choose not to bring your Cocker, you will have to make arrangements for him while you are away. Some options are to take him to a friend's house to stay while you are gone, to have a trusted friend stop by often or stay at your house or to bring your dog to a

A fiberglass crate is needed to transport your dog on an airplane. Oftentimes the airline will supply you with a crate if yours does not meet its requirements.

## COLLAR REQUIRED

If your dog gets lost, he is not able to ask for directions home. Identification tags fastened to the collar give important information—the dog's name, the owner's name, the owner's address and a telephone number where the owner can be reached. This makes it easy for whomever finds the dog to contact the owner and arrange to have the dog returned. An added advantage is that a person will be more likely to approach a lost dog who has ID tags on his collar; it tells the person that this is somebody's pet rather than a stray. This is the easiest and fastest method of identification, provided that the tags stay on the collar and the collar stays on the dog.

reputable boarding kennel. If you choose to board him at a kennel, you should visit in advance to see the facility, how clean it is and where the dogs are kept. Talk to some of the employees and see how they treat the dogs—do they spend time with the dogs, play with them, exercise them, etc.? Also find out the kennel's policy on vaccinations and what they require. This is for all of the dogs' safety, since when dogs are kept together, there is a greater risk of diseases being passed from dog to dog.

Your vet can probably recommend a local kennel in which you can board your Cocker. The kennel should be clean and professionally run, with adequate space for each dog.

## IDENTIFICATION

Your Cocker Spaniel is your valued companion and friend. That is why you always keep a close eye on him and you have made sure that he cannot escape from the yard or wriggle out of his collar and run away from you. However, accidents can happen and there may come a time when your dog unexpectedly gets separated from you. If this unfortunate event should occur, the first thing on your mind will be finding him. Proper identification, including an ID tag and possibly a tattoo and/or microchip, will increase the chances of his being returned to you safely and quickly.

> **TRAVEL TIP**
> When traveling, never let your dog off-lead in a strange area. Your dog could run away out of fear, decide to chase a passing squirrel or cat or simply want to stretch his legs without restriction—if any of these happen, you might never see your canine friend again.

## IDENTIFICATION OPTIONS

As puppies become more and more expensive, especially those puppies of high quality for showing and/or breeding, they have a greater chance of being stolen. The usual collar dog tag is, of course, easily removed. But there are two more permanent techniques that have become widely used for identification.

The puppy microchip implantation involves the injection of a small microchip, about the size of a corn kernel, under the skin of the dog. If your dog shows up at a clinic or shelter, or is offered for resale under less-than-savory circumstances, it can be positively identified by the microchip. The microchip is scanned, and a registry quickly identifies you as the owner.

Tattooing is done on various parts of the dog, from his belly to his ears. The number tattooed can be your telephone number, your dog's registration number or any other number that you can easily memorize. When professional dog thieves see a tattooed dog, they usually lose interest. For the safety of our dogs, no laboratory facility or dog broker will accept a tattooed dog as stock.

Discuss microchipping and tattooing with your veterinarian and breeder. Some vets perform these services on their own premises for a reasonable fee. To ensure that your dog's identification is effective, be certain that the dog is then properly registered with a legitimate national database.

Before your Cocker leaps the fence to chase a passing squirrel or bird, be sure that he is properly identified. At the very least, he needs a collar with his ID tag securely attached.

**Training your Cocker is tantamount to molding his behavior. Cockers live to please their masters. The time you spend training your Cocker will pay off many times over.**

Living with an untrained dog is a lot like owning a piano that you do not know how to play—it is a nice object to look at, but it does not do much more than that to bring you pleasure. Now try taking piano lessons, and suddenly the piano comes alive and brings forth magical sounds and rhythms that set your heart singing and your body swaying.

The same is true with your Cocker Spaniel. Any dog is a big responsibility and, if not trained sensibly, may develop unacceptable behavior that annoys you or could even cause family friction.

To train your Cocker Spaniel, you may like to enroll in an obedience class. Teach him good manners as you learn how and why he behaves the way he

### HONOR AND OBEY
Dogs are the most honorable animals in existence. They consider another species (humans) as their own. They interface with you. You are their leader. Puppies perceive children to be on their level; their actions around small children are different from their behavior around their adult masters.

does. Find out how to communicate with your dog and how to recognize and understand his communications with you. Suddenly the dog takes on a new role in your life—he is smart, interesting, well behaved and fun to be with. He demonstrates his bond of devotion to you daily. In other words, your Cocker Spaniel does wonders for your ego because he constantly reminds you that you are not only his leader, you are his hero!

Those involved with teaching dog obedience and counseling owners about their dogs' behavior have discovered some interesting facts about dog ownership. For example, training dogs when they are puppies results in the highest rate of success in developing well-mannered and well-adjusted adult dogs. Training an older dog, from six months to six years of age, can produce almost equal results, providing that the owner accepts the dog's slower rate of learning capability and is willing to work patiently to help the dog succeed at developing to his fullest potential. Unfortunately, many owners of untrained adult dogs lack the patience factor, so they do not persist until their dogs are successful at learning particular behaviors.

Training a puppy aged 10 to 16 weeks (20 weeks at the most) is like working with a dry sponge in a pool of water. The pup soaks up whatever you show him and constantly looks for more things to do and learn. At this early age, his body is not yet producing hormones, and therein lies the reason for such a high rate of success. Without

**REAP THE REWARDS**
If you start with a normal, healthy dog and give him time, patience and some carefully executed lessons, you will reap the rewards of that training for the life of the dog. And what a life it will be! The two of you will find immeasurable pleasure in the companionship you have built together with love, respect and understanding.

hormones, he is focused on his owners and not particularly interested in investigating other places, dogs, people, etc. You are his leader: his provider of food, water, shelter and security. He latches onto you and wants to stay close. He will usually

**PARENTAL GUIDANCE**

Training a dog is a life experience. Many parents admit that much of what they know about raising children they learned from caring for their dogs. Dogs respond to love, fairness and guidance, just as children do. Become a good dog owner and you may become an even better parent.

Once the puppy begins to produce hormones, his natural curiosity emerges and he begins to investigate the world around him. It is at this time when you may notice that the untrained dog begins to wander away from you and even ignore your commands to stay close. When this behavior becomes a problem, the owner has two choices: get rid of the dog or train him. It is strongly urged that you choose the latter option.

There will usually be obedience classes within a reasonable distance from your home, but you also do a lot to train your dog yourself. Sometimes there are classes available but the tuition is too costly. Whatever the circumstances, the solution to training your Cocker without formal obedience lessons lies within the pages of this book. This chapter is devoted to helping you train your Cocker at home. If the recommended procedures are followed faithfully, you may expect positive results that will prove rewarding to both you and your dog.

Whether your new charge is a puppy or a mature adult, the methods of teaching and the techniques we use in training basic behaviors are the same. After all, no dog, whether puppy or adult, likes harsh or inhumane methods. All creatures, however, respond favorably to

follow you from room to room, will not let you out of his sight when you are outdoors with him and will respond in like manner to the people and animals you encounter. If you greet a friend warmly, he will be happy to greet the person as well. If, however, you are hesitant or anxious about the approach of a stranger, he will respond accordingly.

### MEALTIME

Mealtime should be a peaceful time for your puppy. Do not put his food and water bowls in a high-traffic area in the house. For example, give him his own little corner of the kitchen where he can eat undisturbed and where he will not be underfoot. Do not allow small children or other family members to disturb the pup when he is eating.

Choose an out-of-the-way spot in the yard for your pup's relief area, and bring him there on his leash each time he has "to go."

gentle motivational methods and sincere praise and encouragement. Now let us get started.

### HOUSEBREAKING

You can train a puppy to relieve himself wherever you choose, but this must be somewhere suitable. You should bear in mind from the outset that when your puppy is old enough to go out in public places, any canine deposits must be removed at once. You will always have to carry with you a small plastic bag or "poop-scoop."

Outdoor training includes such surfaces as grass, dirt and

cement. Indoor training usually means training your dog to newspaper. When deciding on the surface and location that you will want your Cocker Spaniel to use, be sure it is going to be permanent. Training your dog to grass and then changing your mind two months later is extremely difficult for both dog and owner.

Next, choose the command you will use each and every time you want your puppy to void. "Hurry up" and "Let's go out" are examples of commands commonly used by dog owners. Get in the habit of giving the puppy your chosen relief command before you take him out. That way, when he becomes an adult, you will be able to determine if he wants to go out when you ask him. A confirmation will be signs of interest, such as wagging his tail, watching you intently, going to the door, etc.

Be a good citizen. Clean up after your dog, even if it is your own yard.

### HOW MANY TIMES A DAY?

| AGE | RELIEF TRIPS |
| --- | --- |
| To 14 weeks | 10 |
| 14–22 weeks | 8 |
| 22–32 weeks | 6 |
| Adulthood | 4 |
| (dog stops growing) | |

These are estimates, of course, but they are a guide to the *minimum* number of opportunities a dog should have each day to relieve himself.

### PUPPY'S NEEDS

Puppy needs to relieve himself after play periods, after each meal, after he has been sleeping and any time he indicates that he is looking for a place to urinate or defecate. The urinary and intestinal tract muscles of very young puppies are not fully developed. Therefore, like human babies, puppies need to relieve themselves frequently.

Take your puppy out often— every hour for an eight-week-old, for example, and always immediately after sleeping and eating. The older the puppy, the less often he will need to relieve himself. Finally, as a mature healthy adult, he will require only three to five relief trips per day.

### HOUSING

Since the types of housing and control you provide for your puppy have a direct relationship on the success of house-training, we consider the various aspects of both before we begin training. Bringing a new puppy home and turning him loose in your house can be compared to turning a child loose in a sports arena and telling the child that the place is all his! The sheer enormity of the place would be too much for him to handle.

Instead, offer the puppy clearly defined areas where he can play, sleep, eat and live. A room of the house where the family gathers is the most obvious choice. Puppies are social animals and need to feel a part of the pack right from the start. Hearing your voice, watching you while you are doing things and smelling you nearby are all positive reinforcers that he is now a member of your pack. Usually a family room, the kitchen or a nearby adjoining breakfast area is ideal for

# Canine Development Schedule

It is important to understand how and at what age a puppy develops into adulthood. If you are a puppy owner, consult the following Canine Development Schedule to determine the stage of development your puppy is currently experiencing. This knowledge will help you as you work with the puppy in the weeks and months ahead.

| Period | Age | Characteristics |
|---|---|---|
| FIRST TO THIRD | BIRTH TO SEVEN WEEKS | Puppy needs food, sleep and warmth, and responds to simple and gentle touching. Needs mother for security and disciplining. Needs littermates for learning and interacting with other dogs. Pup learns to function within a pack and learns pack order of dominance. Begin socializing with adults and children for short periods. Begins to become aware of his environment. |
| FOURTH | EIGHT TO TWELVE WEEKS | Brain is fully developed. Needs socializing with outside world. Remove from mother and littermates. Needs to change from canine pack to human pack. Human dominance necessary. Fear period occurs between 8 and 16 weeks. Avoid fright and pain. |
| FIFTH | THIRTEEN TO SIXTEEN WEEKS | Training and formal obedience should begin. Less association with other dogs, more with people, places, situations. Period will pass easily if you remember this is pup's change-to-adolescence time. Be firm and fair. Flight instinct prominent. Permissiveness and over-disciplining can do permanent damage. Praise for good behavior. |
| JUVENILE | FOUR TO EIGHT MONTHS | Another fear period about 7 to 8 months of age. It passes quickly, but be cautious of fright and pain. Sexual maturity reached. Dominant traits established. Dog should understand sit, down, come and stay by now. |

NOTE: THESE ARE APPROXIMATE TIME FRAMES. ALLOW FOR INDIVIDUAL DIFFERENCES IN PUPPIES.

Your Cocker's crate should have soft, clean bedding upon which he can snuggle and rest comfortably. You want your dog's crate to be a cozy place of retreat and safety.

providing safety and security for both puppy and owner.

Within that room, there should be a smaller area that the puppy can call his own. An alcove, a wire or fiberglass dog crate or a partitioned (not boarded!) corner from which he can view the activities of his new family will be fine. The size of the area or crate is the key factor here. The area must be

large enough for the puppy to lie down and stretch out as well as stand up without rubbing his head on the top, yet small enough so that he cannot relieve himself at one end and sleep at the other without coming into contact with his droppings. Dogs are, by nature, clean animals and will not remain close to their relief areas unless forced to do so. In those cases, they then become dirty dogs and usually remain that way for life.

The designated area should include clean bedding and a toy. Water must always be available, in a non-spill container, although remember that you'll need to be aware of when your pup is drinking water so you'll be able to predict when he will need to relieve himself.

### THE CLEAN LIFE

By providing sleeping and resting quarters that fit the dog, and offering frequent opportunities to relieve himself outside his quarters, the puppy quickly learns that the outdoors (or the newspaper if you are training him to paper) is the place to go when he needs to urinate or defecate. It also reinforces his innate desire to keep his sleeping quarters clean. This, in turn, helps develop the muscle control that will eventually produce a dog with clean living habits.

### CONTROL

By control, we mean helping the puppy to create a lifestyle pattern that will be compatible to that of his human pack (you!). Just as we guide little children to learn our way of life, we must show the puppy when it is time to play, eat, sleep, exercise and even entertain himself.

Your puppy should always sleep in his crate. He should also learn that, during times of household confusion and excessive human activity, such as at breakfast when family members are preparing for the day, he can play by himself in relative safety and comfort in his designated area. Each time you leave the puppy alone, he should understand exactly where he is to stay.

Puppies are chewers. They cannot tell the difference between lamp cords, television wires, shoes, table legs, etc. Chewing into a television wire, for example, can be fatal to the puppy, while a shorted wire can start a fire in the house.

If the puppy chews on the arm of the chair when he is alone, you will probably disci-

# THE SUCCESS METHOD

Success that comes by luck is usually short-lived. Success that comes by well-thought-out proven methods is often more easily achieved and permanent. This is the Success Method. It is designed to give you, the puppy owner, a simple yet proven way to help your puppy develop clean living habits and a feeling of security in his new environment.

## 6 Steps to Successful Crate Training

**1** Tell the puppy "Crate time!" and place him in the crate with a small treat (a piece of cheese or half of a biscuit). Let him stay in the crate for five minutes while you are in the same room. Then release him and praise lavishly. Never release him when he is fussing. Wait until he is quiet before you let him out.

**2** Repeat Step 1 several times a day.

**3** The next day, place the puppy in the crate as before. Let him stay there for ten minutes. Do this several times.

**4** Continue building time in five-minute increments until the puppy stays in his crate for 30 minutes with you in the room. Always take him to his relief area after prolonged periods in his crate.

**5** Now go back to Step 1 and let the puppy stay in his crate for five minutes, this time while you are out of the room.

**6** Once again, build crate time in five-minute increments with you out of the room. When the puppy will stay willingly in his crate (he may even fall asleep!) for 30 minutes with you out of the room, he will be ready to stay in it for several hours at a time.

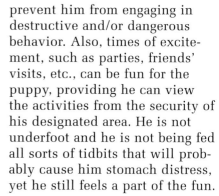

prevent him from engaging in destructive and/or dangerous behavior. Also, times of excitement, such as parties, friends' visits, etc., can be fun for the puppy, providing he can view the activities from the security of his designated area. He is not underfoot and he is not being fed all sorts of tidbits that will probably cause him stomach distress, yet he still feels a part of the fun.

*If your Cocker is waiting by the door, there's a reason! Don't ignore the signs he gives you.*

pline him angrily when you get home. Thus, he makes the association that your coming home means he is going to be punished. (He will not remember chewing the chair and is incapable of making the association of the discipline with his naughty deed.)

The aforementioned scenarios demonstrate examples in which crating the puppy would

### SCHEDULE
A puppy should be taken to his relief area each time he is released from his designated area, after meals, after play sessions and when he first awakens in the morning (at age eight weeks, this can mean 5 a.m.!). The puppy will indicate that he's ready "to go" by circling or sniffing busily—do not misinterpret these signs. For a puppy less than ten weeks of age, a routine of taking him out every hour is necessary. As the puppy grows, he will be able to wait for longer periods of time.

Keep trips to his relief area short. Stay no more than five or six minutes and then return to the house. If he goes during that time, praise him lavishly and take him indoors immediately. If he does not, but he has an accident when you go back indoors, pick him up immediately, say "No! No!" and return to his relief area. Wait a few minutes,

> ### HOUSE-TRAINING TIP
> Most of all, be consistent. Always take your dog to the same location, always use the same command and always have the dog on leash when he is in his relief area, unless a fenced-in yard is available.
>
> By following the Success Method, your puppy will be completely housebroken by the time his muscle and brain development reach maturity. Keep in mind that small breeds usually mature faster than large breeds, but all puppies should be trained by six months of age.

## PLAN TO PLAY

The puppy should also have regular play and exercise sessions when he is with you or a family member. Exercise for a very young puppy can consist of a short walk around the house or yard. Playing can include fetching games with a large ball or a special toy. (All puppies teethe and need soft things upon which to chew.) Remember to restrict play periods to indoors within his living area (the family room, for example) until he is completely house-trained.

then return to the house again. Never hit a puppy or put his face in urine or excrement when he has an accident!

Once indoors, put the puppy in his crate until you have had time to clean up his accident. Then release him to the family area and watch him more closely than before. Chances are, his accident was a result of your not picking up his signal or waiting too long before offering him the opportunity to relieve himself. Never hold a grudge against the puppy for accidents.

Let the puppy learn that going outdoors means it is time to relieve himself, not to play. Once trained, he will be able to play indoors and out and still differentiate between play times and relief times.

Help the pup develop regular hours for naps, being alone, playing by himself and just resting, all in his crate. Encourage him to entertain himself while you are busy with your activities. Let him learn that having you near is comforting, but it is not your main purpose in life to provide him with undivided attention.

Each time you put your puppy in his own area, use the same command, whatever suits best. Soon, he will run to his crate or special area when he hears you say those words. Crate training provides safety for you, the puppy and the home. It also provides the puppy with a feeling of security, and that helps the puppy achieve self-confidence and clean habits.

Remember that one of the primary ingredients in house-training your puppy is control. Regardless of your lifestyle, there will always be occasions when you will need to have a

Crate training makes your Cocker amenable to safe confinement in most any situation: indoors, outdoors, when traveling, etc.

place where your dog can stay and be happy and safe. Crate training is the answer for now and in the future.

In conclusion, a few key elements are really all you need for a successful house-training method—consistency, frequency, praise, control and supervision. By following these procedures with a normal, healthy puppy, you and the puppy will soon be past the stage of "accidents" and ready to move on to a clean and rewarding life together.

## ROLES OF DISCIPLINE, REWARD AND PUNISHMENT

Discipline, training one to act in accordance with rules, brings order to life. It is as simple as that. Without discipline, particularly in a group society, chaos reigns supreme and the group will eventually perish. Humans and canines are social animals and need some form of discipline in order to function effectively. They must procure food, reproduce to keep the species going and protect their home base and their young. If there were no discipline in the lives of social animals, they would eventually die from starvation and/or predation by other stronger animals. In the case of domestic canines, dogs need discipline in their lives in order to understand how their pack (you and other family members)

functions and how they must act in order to survive.

A large humane society in a highly populated area recently surveyed dog owners regarding their satisfaction with their relationships with their dogs. People who had trained their dogs were 75% more satisfied with their pets than those who had never trained their dogs.

Dr. Edward Thorndike, a noted psychologist, established *Thorndike's Theory of Learning*, which states that a behavior that results in a pleasant event tends to be repeated. A behavior that results in an unpleasant event tends not to be repeated. It is this theory on which training methods are based today. For example, if you manipulate a dog to perform a specific behavior and reward him for doing it, he is likely to do it again because he enjoyed the end result.

### COMMAND STANCE
Stand up straight and authoritatively when giving your dog commands. Do not issue commands when lying on the floor or lying on your back on the sofa. You can crouch down to get closer to the Cocker Spaniel's level, but never on all fours. If you are on your hands and knees when you give a command, your dog will think you are positioning yourself to play.

## LANGUAGE BARRIER

Dogs do not understand our language and have to rely on tone of voice more than just words or sound. They can be trained to react to a certain sound, at a certain volume. If you say "No, Oliver" in a very soft, pleasant voice, it will not have the same meaning as "No, Oliver!!" when you raise your voice. You should never use the dog's name during a reprimand, just the command "No! " You never want the dog to associate his name with a negative experience or reprimand.

Occasionally, punishment, a penalty inflicted for an offense, is necessary. The best type of punishment often comes from an outside source. For example, a child is told not to touch the stove because he may get burned. He disobeys and touches the stove. In doing so, he receives a burn. From that time on, he respects the heat of the stove and avoids contact with it. Therefore, a behavior that results in an unpleasant event tends not to be repeated.

A good example of a dog's learning the hard way is the dog who chases the house cat. He is told many times to leave the cat alone, yet he persists in teasing the cat. Then, one day he begins chasing the cat but the cat turns and swipes a claw across the dog's face, leaving him with a painful gash on his nose. The final result is that the dog stops chasing the cat.

## TRAINING EQUIPMENT

### COLLAR AND LEASH

For a Cocker Spaniel, the collar and leash that you use for training must be one with which you are easily able to work, not too heavy for the dog and perfectly safe.

### TREATS

Have a bag of treats on hand. Something nutritious and easy to swallow works best. Use a soft treat, a chunk of cheese or a piece of cooked chicken rather than a dry biscuit. By the time the dog has finished chewing a dry treat, he will forget why he is being rewarded in the first place! Using food rewards will not teach a dog to beg at the table—the only way to teach a dog to beg at the table is to give

Your Cocker must have a collar to which is attached permanent identification tags. The collar must be on the dog securely any time he is outside the home.

him food from the table. In training, rewarding the dog with a food treat will help him associate praise and the treats with learning new behaviors that obviously please his owner.

### TRAINING BEGINS: ASK THE DOG A QUESTION

In order to teach your dog anything, you must first get his attention. After all, he cannot learn anything if he is looking away from you with his mind on something else.

To get his attention, ask him "School?" and immediately walk over to him and give him a treat as you tell him "Good dog." Wait a minute or two and repeat

Produce a treat and all dogs in the house will pay attention! Don't overuse treats, though, or else you could end up with an overweight Cocker who refuses to obey unless bribed to do so.

> **SAFETY FIRST**
> While it may seem that the most important things to your dog are eating, sleeping and chewing the upholstery on your furniture, his first concern is actually safety. The domesticated dogs we keep as companions have the same pack instinct as their ancestors who ran free thousands of years ago. Because of this pack instinct, your dog wants to know that he and his pack are not in danger of being harmed, and that his pack has a strong, capable leader. You must establish yourself as the leader early on in your relationship. That way your dog will trust that you will take care of him and the pack, and he will accept your commands without question.

the routine, this time with a treat in your hand as you approach within a foot of the dog. Do not go directly to him, but stop about a foot short of him and hold out the treat as you ask "School?" He will see you approaching with a treat in your hand and most likely begin walking toward you. As you meet, give him the treat and praise again.

The third time, ask the question, have a treat in your hand and walk only a short distance toward the dog so that he must walk almost all the way to you. As he reaches you, give him the treat and praise again.

By this time, the dog will probably be getting the idea that if he pays attention to you, especially when you ask that question, it will pay off in treats and fun activities for him. In other words, he learns that "school" means doing fun things with you that result in treats and positive attention for him.

Remember that the dog does not understand your verbal language, he only recognizes sounds. Your question translates to a series of sounds for him, and those sounds become the signal to go to you and pay attention; if he does, he will get to interact with you plus receive treats and praise.

## THE BASIC COMMANDS

### TEACHING SIT

Now that you have the dog's attention, attach his leash and hold it in your left hand and a food treat in your right. Place your food hand at the dog's nose and let him lick the treat but not take it from you. Say "Sit" and slowly raise your food hand from in front of the dog's nose up over his head so that he is looking at the ceiling. As he bends his head upward, he will have to bend his knees to maintain his balance. As he bends his knees, he will assume a sit position. At that point, release the

**CALM DOWN**
Dogs will do anything for your attention. If you reward the dog when he is calm and attentive, you will develop a well-mannered dog. If, on the other hand, you greet your dog excitedly and encourage him to wrestle with you, the dog will greet you the same way and you will have a hyperactive dog on your hands.

food treat and praise lavishly with comments such as "Good dog! Good sit!," etc. Remember to always praise enthusiastically, because dogs relish verbal praise from their owners and feel so proud of themselves whenever they accomplish a behavior.

You will not use food forever in getting the dog to obey your commands. Food is only used to teach new behaviors, and once the dog knows what you want when you give a specific command, you will wean him off the food treats but still maintain the verbal praise. After all, you will always have your voice with you, and there will be many times when you have no food rewards but expect the dog to obey.

**TEACHING DOWN**
Teaching the down exercise is easy when you understand how

**DOUBLE JEOPARDY**
A dog in jeopardy never lies down. He stays alert on his feet because instinct tells him that he may have to run away or fight for his survival. Therefore, if a dog feels threatened or anxious, he will not lie down. Consequently, it is important to keep the dog calm and relaxed as he learns the down exercise.

the dog perceives the down position, and it is very difficult when you do not. Dogs perceive the down position as a submissive one; therefore, teaching the down exercise using a forceful method can sometimes make the dog develop such a fear of the down that he either runs away when you say "Down" or he attempts to snap at the person who tries to force him down.

Have the dog sit close alongside your left leg, facing in the same direction as you are. Hold the leash in your left hand and a food treat in your right. Now place your left hand lightly on the top of the dog's shoulders where they meet above the spinal cord. Do not push down on the dog's shoulders; simply rest your left hand there so you can guide the dog to lie down close to your left leg rather than swing away from your side when he drops.

Now place the food hand at the dog's nose, say "Down" very softly (almost a whisper) and slowly lower the food hand to the dog's front feet. When the food hand reaches the floor, begin moving it forward along the floor in front of the dog. Keep talking softly to the dog, saying things like, "Do you want this treat? You can do this, good dog." Your reassuring tone of voice will help calm the dog as he tries to follow the food hand in order to get the treat.

When the dog's elbows touch the floor, release the food and praise softly. Try to get the dog to maintain that down position for several seconds before you let him sit up again. The goal here is to get the dog to settle down and not feel threatened in the down position.

### TEACHING STAY

It is easy to teach the dog to stay in either a sit or a down position. Again, we use food and praise during the teaching process as we help the dog to understand exactly what it is that we are expecting him to do.

To teach the sit/stay, start with the dog sitting on your left side as before and hold the leash in your left hand. Have a food

Owners of show dogs must teach their dog to stay in the standing position, as dogs must stand politely in the ring for extended periods of time while awaiting their turn with the judge.

treat in your right hand and place your food hand at the dog's nose. Say "Stay" and step out on your right foot to stand directly in front of the dog, toe to toe, as he licks and nibbles the treat. Be sure to keep his head facing upward to maintain the sit position. Count to five and then swing around to stand next to the dog again with him on your left. As soon as you get back to the original position, release the food and praise lavishly.

To teach the down/stay, do the down as previously described. As soon as the dog lies down, say "Stay" and step out on your right foot just as you did in the sit/stay. Count to five and then return to stand beside the dog with him on your left

---

## CONSISTENCY PAYS OFF

Dogs need consistency in their feeding schedule, exercise and relief visits, and in the verbal commands you use. If you use "Stay" on Monday and "Stay here, please" on Tuesday, you will confuse your dog. Don't demand perfect behavior during training sessions and then let him have the run of the house the rest of the day. Above all, lavish praise on your pet consistently every time he does something right. The more he feels he is pleasing you, the more willing he will be to learn.

watch the food hand and quickly learn that he is going to get that treat as soon as you return to his side.

When you can stand 3 feet away from your dog for 30 seconds, you can then begin building time and distance in both stays. Eventually, the dog can be expected to remain in the stay position for prolonged periods of time until you return to him or call him to you. Always praise lavishly when he stays.

*Stay can be commanded by voice or hand signal, or a combination of both. Stay is an important command to teach your Cocker, as it gives you control in emergency situations.*

side. Release the treat and praise as always.

Within a week or ten days, you can begin to add a bit of distance between you and your dog when you leave him. When you do, use your left hand open with the palm facing the dog as a stay signal, much the same as the hand signal a police officer uses to stop traffic at an intersection. Hold the food treat in your right hand as before, but this time the food is not touching the dog's nose. He will

### KEEP SMILING
Never train your dog, puppy or adult, when you are angry or in a sour mood. Dogs are very sensitive to human feelings, especially anger, and if your dog senses that you are angry or upset, he will connect your anger with his training and learn to resent or fear his training sessions.

### TEACHING COME
If you make teaching "come" an exciting experience, you should never have a student that does not love the game or that fails to come when called. The secret, it seems, is never to teach the word "come."

At times when an owner most wants his dog to come when called, the owner is likely upset or anxious and he allows these feelings to come through in the tone of his voice when he

*Begin training the stay inside your home where there are few distractions. Once he masters the command indoors, try it outdoors where there are distractions to overcome, such as squirrels, birds, neighbors, etc.*

calls his dog. Hearing that desperation in his owner's voice, the dog fears the results of going to him and therefore either disobeys outright or runs in the opposite direction. The secret, therefore, is to teach the dog a game and, when you want him to come to you, simply play the game. It is practically a no-fail solution!

To begin, have several members of your family take a few food treats and each go into a different room in the house. Take turns calling the dog, and each person should celebrate the dog's finding him with a treat and lots of happy praise. When a person calls the dog, he is actually inviting the dog to find him and get a treat as a reward for "winning."

A few turns of the "Where are you?" game and the dog will figure out that everyone is playing the game and that each person has a big celebration awaiting his success at locating them. Once he learns to love the game, simply calling out "Where are you?" will bring him running from wherever he is when he hears that all-important question.

The come command is recognized as one of the most important things to teach a dog, but there are trainers who work with thousands of dogs and never teach the actual word "Come." Yet these dogs will race to respond to a person who uses the dog's name followed by "Where are you?" For example, a woman has a 12-year-old companion dog who went blind, but who never fails to locate her owner when asked, "Where are you?"

Children particularly love to

Children will enjoy participating in the Cocker's training in whatever aspect possible. This also encourages the dog to behave well with all members of the family.

play this game with their dogs. Children can hide in smaller places like a shower stall or bathtub, behind a bed or under a table. The dog needs to work a little bit harder to find these hiding places, but when he does he loves to celebrate with a treat and a tussle with a favorite youngster.

### TEACHING HEEL

Heeling means that the dog walks beside the owner without pulling. It takes time and patience on the owner's part to succeed at teaching the dog that he (the owner) will not proceed unless the dog is walking calmly beside him. Pulling out ahead on the leash is definitely not acceptable.

Begin with holding the leash in your left hand as the dog sits beside your left leg. Move the loop end of the leash to your right hand but keep your left hand short on the leash so it keeps the dog in close next to you. Say "Heel" and step forward on your left foot. Keep the dog close to you and take three steps. Stop and have the dog sit next to you in what we now call the heel position. Praise verbally, but do not touch the dog. Hesitate a moment and begin again with "Heel," taking three steps and stopping, at which point the dog is told to sit again.

Your goal here is to have the dog walk those three steps without pulling on the leash. When he will walk calmly beside you for three steps without pulling, increase the number of steps you take to five. When he will walk politely beside you while you take five steps, you can increase the length of your walk to ten steps. Keep increasing the length of your stroll until the dog will walk quietly beside you without pulling as long as you want him to heel. When you stop heeling, indicate to the dog that the exercise is over by verbally praising as you pet him and say "OK, good dog." The "OK" is used as a release word, meaning that the exercise is finished and the dog is free to relax.

If you are dealing with a dog who insists on pulling you around, simply "put on your brakes" and stand your

### "COME" . . . BACK

Never call your dog to come to you for a correction or scold him when he reaches you. That is the quickest way to turn a "Come" command into "Go away fast!" Dogs think only in the present tense, and your dog will connect the scolding with coming to you, not with the misbehavior of a few moments earlier.

## FETCH!

Play fetching games with your puppy in an enclosed area where he can retrieve his toy and bring it back to you. Always use a toy or object designated just for this purpose. Never use a shoe, sock or other item he may later confuse with those in your closet or underneath your chair.

ground until the dog realizes that the two of you are not going anywhere until he is beside you and moving at your pace, not his. It may take some time just standing there to convince the dog that you are the leader and you will be the one to decide on the direction and speed of your travel.

Each time the dog looks up at you or slows down to give a

Two dogs participating in a training session means that the owner must have complete control over both dogs, and that each dog is capable of paying attention without being distracted by the other.

Food is used in training new behaviors. Once the dog under-stands what behavior goes with a specific command, it is time to start weaning him off the food treats. At first, give a treat after

### HEELING WELL

Teach your dog to heel in an enclosed area. Once you think the dog will obey reliably and you want to attempt advanced obedience exer-cises such as off-leash heeling, test him in a fenced-in area so he cannot run away.

*Bribery will get you everywhere with a Cocker! Eventually, though, your dog must learn to obey without constant food rewards.*

slack leash between the two of you, quietly praise him and say "Good heel. Good dog." Eventu-ally, the dog will begin to respond and within a few days he will be walking politely beside you without pulling on the leash. At first, the training sessions should be kept short and very positive; soon the dog will be able to walk nicely with you for increasingly longer distances. Remember also to give the dog free time and the oppor-tunity to run and play when you are done with heel practice.

each exercise. Then, start to give a treat only after every other exercise. Mix up the times when you offer a food reward and the times when you only offer praise so that the dog will never know when he is going to receive both food and praise and when he is going to receive only praise. This is called a variable-ratio reward system and it proves successful because there is always the chance that the owner will produce a treat, so the dog never stops trying for that reward. No matter what, *always* give verbal praise.

## OBEDIENCE CLASSES
It is a good idea to enroll in an obedience class if one is available in your area. If yours is a show dog, classes to prepare the two of you for the ring would be more appropriate. Many areas have dog clubs that offer basic obedience training as well as preparatory classes for obedience competition. There are also local dog trainers who offer similar classes.

At obedience trials, dogs can earn titles at various levels of competition. The beginning levels of competition include basic behaviors such as sit, down, heel, etc. The more advanced levels of competition include jumping, retrieving, scent discrimination and signal work. The advanced levels

Heeling is a must for show dogs, who must walk by their handlers' sides for the judge to evaluate their gait. Show Cockers must be under the handler's complete control for the duration of the show.

require a dog and owner to put a lot of time and effort into their training, and the titles that can be earned at these levels of competition are very prestigious.

## OTHER ACTIVITIES FOR LIFE
Whether a dog is trained in the structured environment of a class or alone with his owner at home, there are many activities

### HELPING PAWS
Your dog may not be the next Lassie, but every pet has the potential to do some tricks well. Identify your dog's natural talents and hone them. Is your dog always happy and upbeat? Teach him to wag his tail or give you his paw on command. Real homebodies can be trained to do household chores, such as carrying dirty laundry or retrieving the morning paper.

that can bring fun and rewards to both owner and dog once they have mastered basic control.

Teaching the dog to help out around the home, in the yard or on the farm provides great satisfaction to both dog and owner. In addition, the dog's help makes life a little easier for his owner and raises his stature as a valued companion to his family. It helps give the dog a purpose by occupying his mind and providing an outlet for his energy.

Backpacking is an exciting and healthy activity that the dog can be taught without assistance from more than his owner. The exercise of walking and climbing is good for man and dog alike, and the bond that they develop together is priceless. The rule of

### SCHOOL DAYS
A basic obedience beginner's class usually lasts for six to eight weeks. Dog and owner attend an hour-long lesson once a week and practice for a few minutes, several times a day, each day at home. If done properly, the whole procedure will result in a well-mannered dog and an owner who delights in living with a pet that is eager to please and enjoys doing things with his owner.

thumb is never to let the dog carry more than one-sixth of his body weight.

If you are interested in participating in organized competition with your Cocker performance events that allow him to develop and show off his skills. Many Cockers have achieved high levels of success in field and hunting events, and in tracking tests. To learn more about how to get started, contact the AKC or the American Spaniel Club, which can point you to clubs and events in your area.

Agility is a popular and fun sport where dogs run through an obstacle course that includes various jumps, tunnels and other exercises to test the dog's speed and coordination. The owners run through the course beside their dogs to give commands and to guide them through the course. Although competitive, the focus is on fun—it's fun to do, fun to watch, and great exercise for dog and owner.

Agility trials can be a terrific enjoyment both for you and the Cocker. This Cocker Spaniel named Ashley, owned by John Marmul, is navigating the teeter-totter obstacle.

Spaniel, there are activities other than obedience in which you and your dog can become involved. A sporting spaniel by nature, the Cocker will enjoy training for and competing in

### A BORN PRODIGY

Occasionally, a dog and owner who have not attended formal classes have been able to earn entry-level titles by obtaining competition rules and regulations from a local kennel club and practicing on their own to a degree of perfection. Obtaining the higher level titles, however, almost always requires extensive training under the tutelage of experienced instructors. In addition, the more difficult levels require more specialized equipment whereas the lower levels do not.

Dogs suffer from many of the same physical illnesses as people. They might even share many of the same psychological problems. Since people usually know more about human diseases than canine maladies, many of the terms used in this chapter will be familiar but not necessarily those used by veterinarians. We will use the term *x-ray*, instead of the more acceptable term *radiograph*. We will also use the familiar term *symptoms* even though dogs don't have symptoms, which are verbal descriptions of the patient's feelings: dogs have *clinical signs*. Since dogs can't speak, we have to look for clinical signs...but we still use the term *symptoms* in this book.

As a general rule, medicine is *practiced*. That term is not arbitrary. Medicine is a constantly changing art as we learn more and more about genetics, electronic aids (like CAT scans and MRIs) and daily laboratory advances. There are many dog maladies, like canine hip dysplasia, which are not universally treated in the same manner. For example, some veterinarians opt for surgery more often than others do.

**SELECTING A QUALIFIED VET**
Your selection of a veterinarian should be based upon his personality and skills as well as convenience to your home. You want a vet who is nearby because you might have emergencies or need to make multiple visits for treatments. You want a vet who has services that you might require such as tattooing and boarding facilities, and of course a good reputation for ability and responsiveness. There is nothing more frustrating than having to wait to get a response from your vet.

All veterinarians should be licensed and capable of dealing with routine health issues such as infections, injuries and the promotion of health (for example, by vaccination). Most veterinarians do routine surgery such as neutering, stitching up wounds and docking tails. There are, however, many veterinary specialties that require further studies and internships. For example, there are specialists in heart problems (veterinary cardiologists), skin problems (veterinary dermatologists), teeth and gum problems (veterinary dentists), eye problems (veterinary ophthalmologists) and

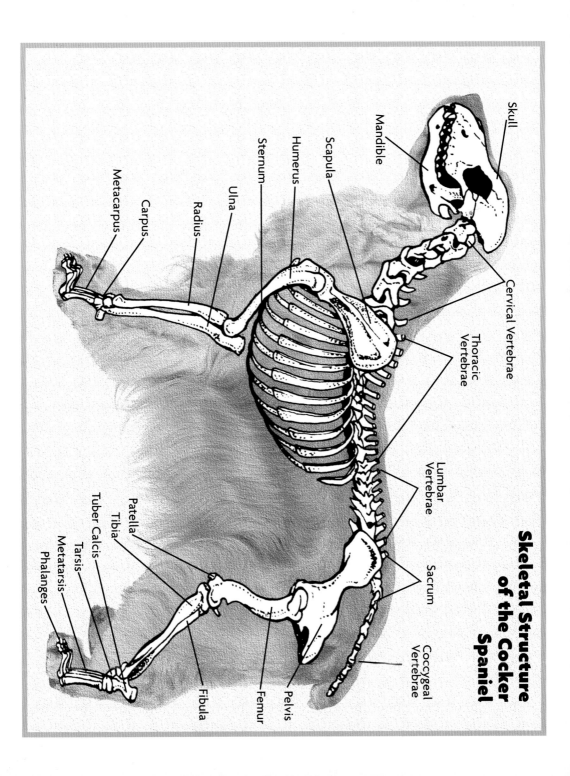

Skeletal Structure
of the Cocker Spaniel

Skull
Mandible
Scapula
Humerus
Sternum
Ulna
Radius
Carpus
Metacarpus
Cervical Vertebrae
Thoracic Vertebrae
Lumbar Vertebrae
Sacrum
Coccygeal Vertebrae
Pelvis
Femur
Fibula
Patella
Tibia
Tuber Calcis
Tarsis
Metatarsis
Phalanges

## Breakdown of Veterinary Income by Category

| | |
|---|---|
| 2% | Dentistry |
| 4% | Radiology |
| 12% | Surgery |
| 15% | Vaccinations |
| 19% | Laboratory |
| 23% | Examinations |
| 25% | Medicines |

A typical vet's income, categorized according to services performed. This survey dealt with small-animal (pets) practices.

x-rays (veterinary radiologists), as well as surgeons who have specialties in bones, muscles or certain organs. If your dog requires the help of a specialist, your vet will refer you to someone in the appropriate field.

When the problem affecting your dog is serious, it is not unusual or impudent to get another medical opinion, although it is courteous to advise the veterinarians concerned about this. You might also want to compare costs among several veterinarians. Sophisticated health care and veterinary services can be very costly. Don't be bashful about discussing these costs with your veterinarian or his staff. If there is more than one treatment option, cost may be a factor in deciding which route to take.

## PREVENTATIVE MEDICINE

It is much easier, less costly and more effective to practice preventative medicine than to fight bouts of illness and disease. Properly bred puppies come from parents that were selected based upon their genetic-disease profiles. Their mother should have been vaccinated, free of all internal and external parasites and properly nourished. For these reasons, a visit to the veterinarian who cared for the dam is recommended. The dam can pass on disease resistance to her puppies, which can last for eight to ten weeks. She can also pass on parasites and many infections. That's why it's helpful to know as much as possible about the dam's health.

**WEANING TO BRINGING PUPPY HOME**
Puppies should be weaned by the time they are about two months old. A puppy that remains for at

### PUPPY VACCINATIONS

Your veterinarian will probably recommend that your puppy be fully vaccinated before you take him outside. There are airborne diseases, parasite eggs in the grass and unexpected visits from other dogs that might be dangerous to your puppy's health. Other dogs are the most harmful reservoir of pathogenic organisms, as everything they have can be transmitted to your puppy.

 # First Aid at a Glance

## Burns
Place the affected area under cool water; use ice if only a small area is burnt.

## Bee stings/Insect bites
Apply ice to relieve swelling; antihistamine dosed properly.

## Animal bites
Clean any bleeding area; apply pressure until bleeding subsides; go to the vet.

## Spider bites
Use cold compress and a pressurized pack to inhibit venom's spreading.

## Antifreeze poisoning
Immediately induce vomiting by using hydrogen peroxide.

## Fish hooks
Removal best handled by vet; hook must be cut in order to remove.

## Snake bites
Pack ice around bite; contact vet quickly; identify snake for proper antivenin.

## Car accident
Move dog from roadway with blanket; seek veterinary aid.

## Shock
Calm the dog; keep him warm; seek immediate veterinary help.

## Nosebleed
Apply cold compress to the nose; apply pressure to any visible abrasion.

## Bleeding
Apply pressure above the area; treat wound by applying a cotton pack.

## Heat stroke
Submerge dog in cold bath; cool down with fresh air and water; go to the vet.

## Frostbite/Hypothermia
Warm the dog with a warm bath, electric blankets or hot water bottles.

## Abrasions
Clean the wound and wash out thoroughly with fresh water; apply antiseptic.

 *Remember: an injured dog may attempt to bite a helping hand from fear and confusion. Always muzzle the dog before trying to offer assistance.*

## HEALTH AND VACCINATION SCHEDULE

| Age in Weeks: | 3RD | 6TH | 8TH | 10TH | 12TH | 14TH | 16TH | 20-24TH |
|---|---|---|---|---|---|---|---|---|
| Worm Control | ✔ | ✔ | ✔ | ✔ | ✔ | ✔ | ✔ | ✔ |
| Neutering | | | | | | | | ✔ |
| Heartworm | | ✔ | | | | | | ✔ |
| Parvovirus | | ✔ | | ✔ | | ✔ | | ✔ |
| Distemper | | | ✔ | | ✔ | | ✔ | |
| Hepatitis | | | ✔ | | ✔ | | ✔ | |
| Leptospirosis | | ✔ | | ✔ | | ✔ | | |
| Parainfluenza | | ✔ | | ✔ | | ✔ | | |
| Dental Examination | | | ✔ | | | | | ✔ |
| Complete Physical | | | ✔ | | | | | ✔ |
| Temperament Testing | | | ✔ | | | | | |
| Coronavirus | | | | | ✔ | | | |
| Canine Cough | | ✔ | | | | | | |
| Hip Dysplasia | | | | | | | ✔ | |
| Rabies | | | | | | | | ✔ |

Vaccinations are not instantly effective. It takes about two weeks for the dog's immune system to develop antibodies. Most vaccinations require annual booster shots. Your veterinarian should guide you in this regard.

least eight weeks with his mother and littermates usually adapts better to other dogs and people later in life.

Sometimes new owners have their puppy examined by a veterinarian immediately, which is a good idea unless the puppy is overtired by the journey home. In that case, an appointment should be arranged for the next day.

The puppy will have his teeth examined and have his skeletal conformation and general health checked prior to certification by the veterinarian. Puppies in certain breeds have problems with their kneecaps, cataracts and other eye problems, heart murmurs and undescended testicles. Your veterinarian might also have training in temperament testing and evaluation. At the first visit, the vet will set up a schedule for the pup's vaccinations.

### VACCINATION SCHEDULING
Most vaccinations are given by injection and should only be done by a veterinarian. Both he and you should keep a record of the date of the injection, the identification of the vaccine and the amount given. Some vets give a first vaccination

## VACCINE ALLERGIES

Vaccines do not work all the time. Sometimes dogs are allergic to them and many times the antibodies, which are supposed to be stimulated by the vaccine, just are not produced. You should keep your dog in the veterinary clinic for an hour after it is vaccinated to be sure there are no allergic reactions.

ing is usually based on a two- to four-week cycle. You must take your vet's advice as to when to vaccinate, as this may differ according to the vaccine used.

Most vaccinations immunize your puppy against viruses. The usual vaccines contain immunizing doses of several different viruses such as distemper, parvovirus, parainfluenza and hepatitis. There are other vaccines available when the puppy is at risk. You should rely upon professional advice. This is especially true for the booster-shot program. Most vaccination programs require a booster when the puppy is a year old and once a year there-

at six weeks, but most dog breeders prefer the course not to commence until about eight weeks because of the risk of negating any antibodies passed on by the dam. The vaccination schedul-

| Disease | What is it? | What causes it? | Symptoms |
|---------|-------------|-----------------|----------|
| **Leptospirosis** | Severe disease that affects the internal organs; can be spread to people. | A bacterium, which is often carried by rodents, that enters through mucous membranes and spreads quickly throughout the body. | Range from fever, vomiting and loss of appetite in less severe cases to shock, irreversible kidney damage and possibly death in most severe cases. |
| **Rabies** | Potentially deadly virus that infects warm-blooded mammals. | Bite from a carrier of the virus, mainly wild animals. | 1st stage: dog exhibits change in behavior, fear. 2nd stage: dog's behavior becomes more aggressive. 3rd stage: loss of coordination, trouble with bodily functions. |
| **Parvovirus** | Highly contagious virus, potentially deadly. | Ingestion of the virus, which is usually spread through the feces of infected dogs. | Most common: severe diarrhea. Also vomiting, fatigue, lack of appetite. |
| **Canine cough** | Contagious respiratory infection. | Combination of types of bacteria and virus. Most common: *Bordetella bronchiseptica* bacteria and parainfluenza virus. | Chronic cough. |
| **Distemper** | Disease primarily affecting respiratory and nervous system. | Virus that is related to the human measles virus. | Mild symptoms such as fever, lack of appetite and mucus secretion progress to evidence of brain damage, "hard pad." |
| **Hepatitis** | Virus primarily affecting the liver. | Canine adenovirus type I (CAV-I). Enters system when dog breathes in particles. | Lesser symptoms include listlessness, diarrhea, vomiting. More severe symptoms include "blue-eye" (clumps of virus in eye). |
| **Coronavirus** | Virus resulting in digestive problems. | Virus is spread through infected dog's feces. | Stomach upset evidenced by lack of appetite, vomiting, diarrhea. |

## PET ADVANTAGES

If you do not intend to show or breed your new puppy, your veterinarian will probably recommend that you spay your female or neuter your male. Some people believe neutering leads to weight gain, but if you feed and exercise your dog properly, this is easily avoided. Spaying or neutering can actually have many positive outcomes, such as:

- training becomes easier, as the dog focuses less on the urge to mate and more on you!
- females are protected from unplanned pregnancy as well as ovarian and uterine cancers.
- males are guarded from testicular tumors and have a reduced risk of developing prostate cancer.

Talk to your vet regarding the right age to spay/neuter and other aspects of the procedure.

puppy around six months of age is recommended. Discuss this with your vet; most professionals advise having this done. Neutering/spaying has proven to be extremely beneficial to male and female puppies, respectively. Besides eliminating the possibility of pregnancy and pyometra in bitches and testicular cancer in males, it also greatly reduces the risk of (but does not prevent) breast cancer in bitches and prostate cancer in male dogs.

### DOGS OLDER THAN ONE YEAR

Continue to visit the veterinarian at least once a year. There is no such disease as old age, but bodily functions do change with age. The eyes and ears are no longer as efficient. Liver, kidney and intestinal functions often decline. Proper dietary changes, recommended by your veterinarian, can make life more pleasant for the aging Cocker Spaniel and you.

## SKIN PROBLEMS IN COCKER SPANIELS

Veterinarians are consulted by dog owners for skin problems more than for any other group of diseases or maladies. Dogs' skin is almost as sensitive as human skin and both can suffer from almost the same ailments (though the occurrence of acne in most dogs is rare). For this reason, veterinary dermatology has

after. In some cases, circumstances may require more or less frequent immunizations. Canine cough, more formally known as tracheobronchitis, is treated with a vaccine that is sprayed into the dog's nostrils. Canine cough is usually included in routine vaccination, but is often not as effective as other major vaccines.

### FIVE MONTHS TO ONE YEAR OF AGE

Unless you intend to breed or show your dog, neutering the

# Internal Organs with Skeletal Structure

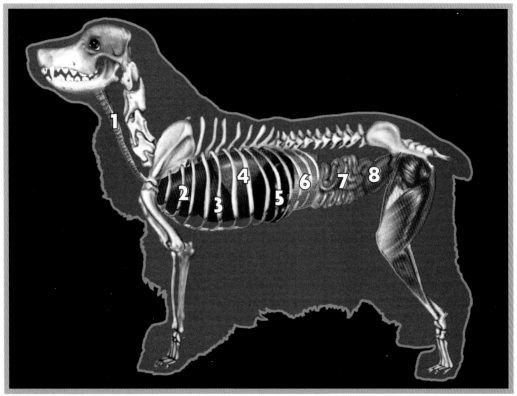

1. Esophagus  2. Lungs  3. Gall Bladder  4. Liver  5. Kidney  6. Stomach  7. Intestines  8. Urinary Bladder

developed into a specialty practiced by many veterinarians.

Since many skin problems have visual symptoms that are almost identical, it requires the skill of an experienced veterinary dermatologist to identify and cure many of the more severe skin disorders. Pet shops sell many treatments for skin problems, but most of the treatments

**MANY KINDS OF EARS**

Not every dog's ears are the same. Ears that are open to the air are healthier than ears with poor air circulation. Sometimes a dog can have two differently shaped ears. You should not probe inside your dog's ears. Only clean that which is accessible with a cotton ball.

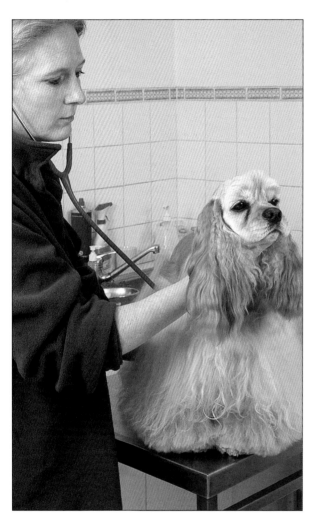

Next to you, your veterinarian will be your Cocker Spaniel's best friend!

### HEREDITARY SKIN DISORDERS

Veterinary dermatologists are currently researching a number of skin disorders that are believed to have hereditary bases. These inherited diseases are transmitted by both parents, who appear (phenotypically) normal but have a recessive gene for the disease, meaning that they carry, but are not affected by, the disease. These diseases pose serious problems to breeders because in some instances there are no methods of identifying carriers. Often the secondary diseases associated with these skin conditions are even more debilitating than the skin disorders themselves, including cancers and respiratory problems.

Among the hereditary skin disorders for which the mode of inheritance is known are acrodermatitis, cutaneous asthenia (Ehlers-Danlos syndrome), sebaceous adenitis, cyclic hematopoiesis, dermatomyositis, IgA deficiency, color dilution alopecia and nodular dermatofibrosis. Some of these disorders are limited to one or two breeds, while others affect a large number of breeds. All inherited diseases must be diagnosed and treated by a veterinary specialist.

are directed at symptoms and not the underlying problem(s). If your dog is suffering from a skin disorder, you should seek professional assistance as quickly as possible. As with all diseases, the earlier a problem is identified and treated, the more likely it is that the cure will be successful.

### PARASITE BITES

Many of us are allergic to insect bites. The bites itch, erupt and may even become infected. Dogs have the same reaction to fleas, ticks and/or mites. When an insect lands on you, you have the chance to whisk it away with your hand. Unfortunately, when our dog is bitten by a flea, tick or mite, he can only scratch it away or bite it. By the time the dog has been bitten, the parasite has done some of its damage. It may also have laid eggs, which will cause further problems in the near future. The itching from parasite bites is probably due to the saliva injected into the site when the parasite sucks the dog's blood.

### ACRAL LICK GRANULOMA AND HOT SPOTS

Many dogs have a very poorly understood syndrome called acral lick granuloma. The manifestation of the problem is the dog's tireless attack at a specific area of the body, almost always the legs or paws. The dog licks so intensively that he removes the hair and skin, leaving an ugly, large wound. Tiny protuberances, which are outgrowths of new capillaries, bead on the surface of the wound. Owners who notice their dogs' biting and chewing at their extremities should have the vet determine the cause. If lick granuloma is identified, although there is no absolute cure, corticosteroids are the most common treatment.

Similarly, hot spots, also called moist dermatitis, affect the Cocker in warm weather. These patches are usually found on the hindquarters, tail or trunk, bald from the dog's licking at them. They can be treated with corticosteroids by a vet. Owners should keep dogs well groomed in the warm months and always dry the dog thoroughly after a bath, especially the tail area and hindquarters.

### AIRBORNE ALLERGIES

An interesting allergy is pollen allergy. Humans have hay fever, rose fever and other fevers with which they suffer during the pollinating season. Many dogs suffer the same allergies. When the pollen count is high, your dog might suffer, but don't expect him to sneeze and

**BE CAREFUL WHERE YOU WALK YOUR DOG**

Dogs who have been exposed to lawns sprayed with herbicides have double and triple the rate of malignant lymphoma. Suburban dogs are especially at risk, as they are exposed to manicured lawns and gardens. Dogs perspire and absorb through their footpads. Be careful where your dog walks and always avoid any area that appears yellowed from chemical overspray. These chemicals are not good for you, either!

have a runny nose like a human would. Dogs react to pollen allergies the same way they react to fleas—they scratch and bite themselves.

Dogs, like humans, can be tested for allergens. Discuss the testing with your veterinary dermatologist.

### CARETAKER OF TEETH

You are your dog's caretaker and his dentist. Vets warn that plaque and tartar buildup on the teeth will damage the gums and allow bacteria to enter the dog's bloodstream, causing serious damage to the animal's vital organs. Studies show that over 50 percent of dogs have some form of gum disease before age three. Daily or weekly tooth cleaning (with a brush or soft gauze pad wipes) can add to your dog's life.

## AUTO-IMMUNE ILLNESSES

An auto-immune illness is one in which the immune system over-acts and does not recognize parts of the affected person or dog; rather, the immune system starts to react as if these parts were foreign and need to be destroyed. An example is rheumatoid arthritis, which occurs when the body does not recognize the joints, thus leading to a very painful and damaging reaction in the joints. This has nothing to do with age, so can occur in children and young dogs. The wear-and-tear arthritis of the older person or dog is osteoarthritis.

Lupus is an auto-immune disease that affects dogs as well as people. It can take variable forms, affecting the kidneys, bones and the skin. It can be fatal, so is treated with steroids, which can themselves have very significant side effects. The steroids calm down the allergic reaction to the body's tissues, which helps the lupus, but the steroids also calm down the body's reaction to real foreign substances such as bacteria, and also thin the skin and bones.

## FOOD PROBLEMS

### Food Allergies

Some dogs can be allergic to foods that may be best-sellers and highly recommended by breeders and vets. Changing the brand of

food that you buy may not eliminate the problem if the element
to which the dog is allergic is
contained in the new brand.

Recognizing a food allergy in
a dog can be difficult. Humans
often have rashes when they eat
foods to which they are allergic,
or have swelling of the lips or
eyes. Dogs do not usually
develop rashes, but react in the
same way as they do to an
airborne or bite allergy—they
itch, scratch and bite. While
pollen allergies are usually
seasonal, food allergies are year-
round problems.

### TREATING FOOD ALLERGY

Diagnosis of food allergy is based
on a two- to four-week dietary
trial with a home-cooked diet fed
to the exclusion of all other
foods. The diet should consist of
boiled rice or potato with a
source of protein that the dog has
never eaten before, such as fresh
or frozen fish, lamb or even
something as exotic as pheasant
or ostrich (if this is not too
expensive in your part of the
country). Water has to be the
only drink, and it is really important that no other foods are fed
during this trial. If the dog's
condition improves, you will
need to try the original diet once
again to see if the itching
resumes. If it does, then this
confirms the diagnosis that the
dog is allergic to his original diet.

**THE SAME ALLERGIES**
Chances are that you and your dog
will have the same allergies. Your
allergies are readily recognizable and
usually easily treated. Your dog's allergies may be masked.

The treatment is long-term feeding of something that does not
distress the dog's skin, which
may be in the form of one of the
commercially available hypoallergenic diets or the home-made
diet that you created for the
allergy trial.

### FOOD INTOLERANCE

Food intolerance is the inability
of the dog to completely digest
certain foods. This occurs
because the dog does not have
the chemicals necessary to digest
some foodstuffs. These chemicals
are called enzymes. All puppies
have the enzymes necessary to
digest canine milk, but some
dogs do not have the enzymes to
digest a very different form of
milk that is commonly found in
human households—milk from
cows. In such dogs, drinking
cows' milk results in loose
bowels, stomach pains and the
passage of gas.

Dogs often do not have the
enzymes to digest soy or other
beans. The treatment is to
exclude the foodstuffs that upset
your Cocker Spaniel's digestion.

A male dog flea, *Ctenocephalides canis.*

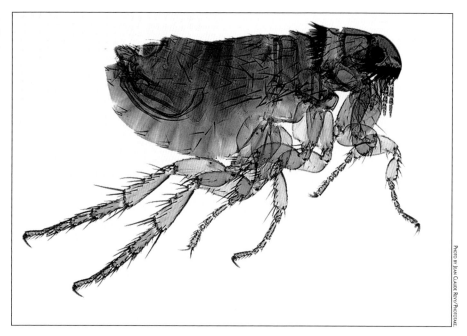

PHOTO BY JEAN CLAUDE REVY/PHOTOTAKE

## EXTERNAL PARASITES

### FLEAS

Of all the problems to which dogs are prone, none is more well known and frustrating than fleas. Flea infestation is relatively simple to cure but difficult to prevent. Parasites that are harbored inside the body are a bit more difficult to eradicate but they are easier to control.

To control flea infestation, you have to understand the flea's life cycle. Fleas are often thought of as a summertime problem, but centrally heated homes have changed the patterns and fleas can be found at any time of the year. The most effective method of flea control is a two-stage approach: one stage to kill the adult fleas, and the other to control the development of pre-adult fleas. Unfortunately, no single active ingredient is effective against all stages of the life cycle.

### FLEA KILLER CAUTION—"POISON"

Flea-killers are poisonous. You should not spray these toxic chemicals on areas of a dog's body that he licks, including his genitals and his face. Flea killers taken internally are a better answer, but check with your vet in case internal therapy is not advised for your dog.

### LIFE CYCLE STAGES

During its life, a flea will pass through four life stages: egg, larva, pupa or nymph and adult. The adult stage is the most visible and irritating stage of the flea life cycle, and this is why the majority of flea-control products concentrate on this stage. The fact is that adult fleas account for only 1% of the total flea population, and the other 99% exist in pre-adult stages, i.e., eggs, larvae and nymphs. The pre-adult stages are barely visible to the naked eye.

### THE LIFE CYCLE OF THE FLEA

Eggs are laid on the dog, usually in quantities of about 20 or 30, several times a day. The adult female flea must have a blood meal before each egg-laying session. When first laid, the eggs will cling to the dog's hair, as the eggs are still moist. However, they will quickly dry out and fall from the dog, especially if the dog moves around or scratches. Many eggs will fall off in the dog's favorite area or an area in which he spends a lot of time, such as his bed.

Once the eggs fall from the dog onto the carpet or furniture, they will hatch into larvae. This takes from one to ten days. Larvae are not particularly mobile and will usually travel only a few inches from where they hatch. However, they do have a tendency to move away from bright light and heavy

***EN GARDE:***
**CATCHING FLEAS OFF GUARD!**
Consider the following ways to arm yourself against fleas:
- Add a small amount of pennyroyal or eucalyptus oil to your dog's bath. These natural remedies repel fleas.
- Supplement your dog's food with fresh garlic (minced or grated) and a hearty amount of brewer's yeast, both of which ward off fleas.
- Use a flea comb on your dog daily. Submerge fleas in a cup of bleach to kill them quickly.
- Confine the dog to only a few rooms to limit the spread of fleas in the home.
- Vacuum daily...and get all of the crevices! Dispose of the bag every few days until the problem is under control.
- Wash your dog's bedding daily. Cover cushions where your dog sleeps with towels, and wash the towels often.

traffic—under furniture and behind doors are common places to find high quantities of flea larvae.

The flea larvae feed on dead organic matter, including adult flea feces, until they are ready to change into adult fleas. Fleas will usually remain as larvae for around seven days. After this period, the larvae will pupate into protective pupae. While inside the pupae, the larvae will undergo

Fleas have been measured as being able to jump 300,000 times and can jump over 150 times their length in any direction, including straight up.

metamorphosis and change into adult fleas. This can take as little time as a few days, but the adult fleas can remain inside the pupae waiting to hatch for up to two years. The pupae are signaled to hatch by certain stimuli, such as physical pressure—the pupae's being stepped on, heat from an animal's lying on the pupae or increased carbon-dioxide levels and vibrations—indicating that a suitable host is available.

Once hatched, the adult flea must feed within a few days. Once the adult flea finds a host, it will not leave voluntarily. It only becomes dislodged by grooming or the host animal's scratching.

The adult flea will remain on the host for the duration of its life unless forcibly removed.

### TREATING THE ENVIRONMENT AND THE DOG

Treating fleas should be a two-pronged attack. First, the environment needs to be treated; this includes carpets and furniture, especially the dog's bedding and areas underneath furniture. The environment should be treated with a household spray containing an Insect Growth Regulator (IGR) and an insecticide to kill the adult fleas. Most IGRs are effective against eggs and larvae; they actually mimic the fleas' own hormones and stop the eggs and larvae from developing into adult fleas. There are currently no treatments available to attack the pupa stage of the life cycle, so the adult insecticide is used to kill the newly hatched adult fleas before they find a host. Most IGRs are active for many months, while

A scanning electron micrograph of a dog or cat flea, *Ctenocephalides,* magnified more than 100x. This image has been colorized for effect.

# THE LIFE CYCLE OF THE FLEA

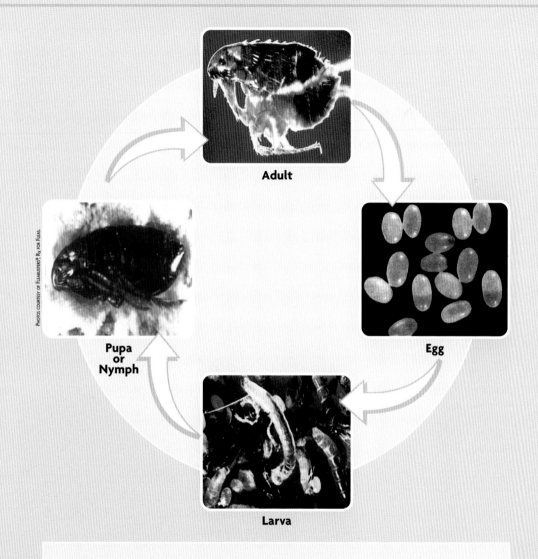

Adult

Egg

Larva

Pupa
or
Nymph

Fleas have been around for millions of years and have adapted to changing host animals. They are able to go through a complete life cycle in less than one month or they can extend their lives to almost two years by remaining as pupae or cocoons. They do not need blood or any other food for up to 20 months.

### INSECT GROWTH REGULATOR

Two types of products should be used when treating fleas—a product to treat the pet and a product to treat the home. Adult fleas represent less than 1% of the flea population. The pre-adult fleas (eggs, larvae and pupae) represent more than 99% of the flea population and are found in the environment; it is in the case of pre-adult fleas that products containing an Insect Growth Regulator (IGR) should be used in the home.

IGRs are a new class of compounds used to prevent the development of insects. They do not kill the insect outright, but instead use the insect's biology against it to stop it from completing its growth. Products that contain methoprene are the world's first and leading IGRs. Used to control fleas and other insects, this type of IGR will stop flea larvae from developing and protect the house for up to seven months.

The American dog tick, *Dermacentor variabilis*, is probably the most common tick found on dogs. Look at the strength in its eight legs! No wonder it's hard to detach them.

adult insecticides are only active for a few days.

When treating with a household spray, it is a good idea to vacuum before applying the product. This stimulates as many pupae as possible to hatch into adult fleas. The vacuum cleaner should also be treated with an insecticide to prevent the eggs and larvae that have been collected in the vacuum bag from hatching.

The second stage of treatment is to apply an adult insecticide to the dog. Traditionally, this would be in the form of a collar or a spray, but more recent innovations include digestible insecticides that poison the fleas when they ingest the dog's blood. Alternatively, there are drops that, when placed on the back of the dog's neck, spread throughout the hair and skin to kill adult fleas.

### TICKS

Though not as common as fleas, ticks are found all over the tropical and temperate world. They don't bite, like fleas; they harpoon. They dig their sharp proboscis (nose) into the dog's skin and drink the blood. Their

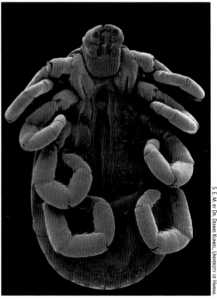

only food and drink is dog's blood. Dogs can get Lyme disease, Rocky Mountain spotted fever, tick bite paralysis and many other diseases from ticks. They may live where fleas are found and they like to hide in cracks or seams in walls. They are controlled the same way fleas are controlled.

The American dog tick, *Dermacentor variabilis*, may well be the most common dog tick in many geographical areas, especially those areas where the climate is hot and humid. Most dog ticks have life expectancies of a week to six months, depending upon climatic conditions. They can neither jump nor fly, but they can crawl slowly and can range up to 16 feet to reach a sleeping or unsuspecting dog.

## MITES

Just as fleas and ticks can be problematic for your dog, mites can also lead to an itchy nuisance. Microscopic in size, mites are related to ticks and generally take up permanent residence on their host animal— in this case, your dog! The term *mange* refers to any infestation caused by one of the mighty mites, of which there are six varieties that concern dog owners.

*Demodex* mites cause a condition known as demodicosis

### DEER-TICK CROSSING

The great outdoors may be fun for your dog, but it also is a home to dangerous ticks. Deer ticks carry a bacterium known as *Borrelia burgdorferi* and are most active in the autumn and spring. When infections are caught early, penicillin and tetracycline are effective antibiotics, but, if left untreated, the bacteria may cause neurological, kidney and cardiac problems as well as long-term trouble with walking and painful joints.

PHOTO BY DR. DENNIS KUNKEL, UNIVERSITY OF HAWAII

The head of an American dog tick, *Dermacentor variabilis*, enlarged and colorized for effect.

The mange mite, *Psoroptes bovis*, can infest cattle and other domestic animals.

PHOTO BY JAMES HAYDEN/YOAV/PHOTOTAKE

Human lice look like dog lice; the two are closely related.

PHOTO BY DWIGHT R. KUHN.

(sometimes called red mange or follicular mange), in which the mites live in the dog's hair follicles and sebaceous glands in larger-than-normal amounts. This type of mange is commonly passed from the dam to her puppies and usually shows up on the puppies' muzzles, though demodicosis is not transferable from one normal dog to another. Most dogs recover from this type of mange without any treatment, though topical therapies are commonly prescribed by the vet.

The *Cheyletiellosis* mite is the hook-mouthed culprit associated with "walking dandruff," a condition that affects dogs as well as cats and rabbits. This mite lives on the surface of the animal's skin and is readily transferable through direct or indirect contact with an affected animal. The dandruff is present in the form of scaly skin, which may or may not be itchy. If not treated, this mange can affect a whole kennel of dogs and can be spread to humans as well.

The *Sarcoptes* mite causes intense itching on the dog in the form of a condition known as scabies or sarcoptic mange. The cycle of the *Sarcoptes* mite lasts about three weeks, and the mites live in the top layer of the dog's skin (epidermis), preferably in areas with little hair. Scabies is highly contagious and can be passed to humans. Sometimes an allergic reaction to the mite worsens the severe itching associated with sarcoptic mange.

Ear mites, *Otodectes cynotis,* lead to otodectic mange, which most commonly affects the outer ear canal of the dog, though other areas can be affected as well. Dogs with ear-mite infestation commonly scratch at their ears, causing further irritation, and shake their heads. Dark brown droppings in the outer ear confirm the diagnosis. Your vet can prescribe a treatment to flush out the ears and kill any eggs in the ears. A complete month of treatment is necessary to cure the mange.

Two other mites, less common in dogs, include *Dermanyssus gallinae* (the poultry or red mite) and *Eutrombicula alfreddugesi* (the North American mite associated with trombiculidiasis or chigger infestation). The poultry mite frequently lives on chickens, but can transfer to dogs who spend time near farm animals. Chigger

---

**DO NOT MIX**
Never mix parasite-control products without first consulting your vet. Some products can become toxic when combined with others and can cause fatal consequences.

---

**NOT A DROP TO DRINK**
Never allow your dog to swim in polluted water or public areas where water quality can be suspect. Even perfectly clear water can harbor parasites, many of which can cause serious to fatal illnesses in canines. Areas inhabited by water-fowl and other wildlife are especially dangerous.

---

infestation affects dogs in the Central US who have exposure to woodlands. The types of mange caused by both of these mites are treatable by veterinarians.

### INTERNAL PARASITES

Most animals—fishes, birds and mammals, including dogs and humans—have worms and other parasites that live inside their bodies. According to Dr. Herbert R. Axelrod, the fish pathologist, there are two kinds of parasites: dumb and smart. The smart parasites live in peaceful cooperation with their hosts (symbiosis), while the dumb parasites kill their hosts. Most worm infections are relatively easy to control. If they are not controlled, they weaken the host dog to the point that other medical problems occur, but they do not kill the host as dumb parasites would.

A brown dog tick, *Rhipicephalus sanguineus,* is an uncommon but annoying tick found on dogs.

Photo by Carolina Biological Supply/Phototake.

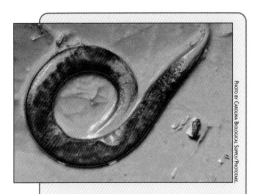

Photo by Carolina Biological Supply/Phototake.

The roundworm *Rhabditis* can infect both dogs and humans.

The roundworm, *Ascaris lumbricoides.*

## ROUNDWORMS

Average-size dogs can pass 1,360,000 roundworm eggs every day. For example, if there were only 1 million dogs in the world, the world would be saturated with thousands of tons of dog feces. These feces would contain around 15,000,000,000 roundworm eggs.

Up to 31% of home yards and children's sand boxes in the US contain roundworm eggs.

Flushing dog's feces down the toilet is not a safe practice because the usual sewage treatments do not destroy roundworm eggs.

Infected puppies start shedding roundworm eggs at three weeks of age. They can be infected by their mother's milk.

## ROUNDWORMS

The roundworms that infect dogs are known scientifically as *Toxocara canis.* They live in the dog's intestines and shed eggs continually. It has been estimated that a dog produces about 6 or more ounces of feces every day. Each ounce of feces averages hundreds of thousands of roundworm eggs. There are no known areas in which dogs roam that do not contain roundworm eggs. The greatest danger of roundworms is that they infect people, too! It is wise to have your dog tested regularly for roundworms.

In young puppies, roundworms cause bloated bellies, diarrhea, coughing and vomiting, and are transmitted from the dam (through blood or milk). Affected puppies will not appear as animated as normal puppies. The worms appear spaghetti-like, measuring as long as 6 inches. Adult dogs can acquire roundworms through coprophagia (eating contaminated feces) or by killing rodents that carry roundworms.

Roundworm infection can kill puppies and cause severe problems in adults, as the hatched larvae travel to the lungs and trachea through the bloodstream. Cleanliness is the best preventative for roundworms. Always pick up after your dog and dispose of feces in appropriate receptacles.

Photo by Dwight R. Kuhn.

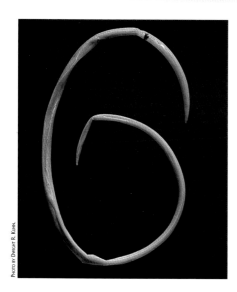

## HOOKWORMS

In the United States, dog owners have to be concerned about four different species of hookworm, the most common and most serious of which is *Ancylostoma caninum,* which prefers warm climates. The others are *Ancylostoma braziliense, Ancylostoma tubaeforme* and *Uncinaria stenocephala,* the latter of which is a concern to dogs living in the Northern US and Canada, as this species prefers cold climates. Hookworms are dangerous to humans as well as to dogs and cats, and can be the cause of severe anemia due to iron deficiency. The worm uses its teeth to attach itself to the dog's intestines and changes the site of its attachment about six times per day. Each time the worm repositions itself, the dog loses blood and can become anemic. *Ancylostoma caninum* is the most likely of the four species to cause anemia in the dog.

Symptoms of hookworm infection include dark stools, weight loss, general weakness, pale coloration and anemia, as well as possible skin problems. Fortunately, hookworms are easily purged from the affected dog with a number of medications that have proven effective. Discuss these with your veterinarian. Most heartworm preventatives include a hookworm insecticide as well.

Owners also must be aware that hookworms can infect humans, who can acquire the larvae through exposure to contaminated feces. Since the worms cannot complete their life cycle on a human, the worms simply infest the skin and cause irritation. This condition is known as cutaneous larva migrans syndrome. As a preventative, use disposable gloves or a "poop-scoop" to pick up your dog's droppings and prevent your dog (or neighborhood cats) from defecating in children's play areas.

The hookworm, *Ancylostoma caninum.*

The infective stage of the hookworm larva.

## TAPEWORMS

Humans, rats, squirrels, foxes, coyotes, wolves and domestic dogs are all susceptible to tapeworm infection. Except in humans, tapeworms are usually not a fatal infection. Infected individuals can harbor 1000 parasitic worms.

Tapeworms, like some other types of worm, are hermaphroditic, meaning male and female in the same worm.

If dogs eat infected rats or mice, or anything else infected with tapeworm, they get the tapeworm disease. One month after attaching to a dog's intestine, the worm starts shedding eggs. These eggs are infective immediately. Infective eggs can live for a few months without a host animal.

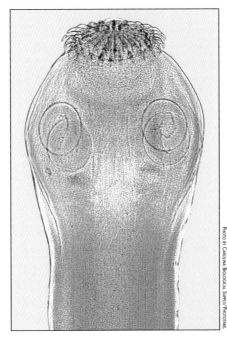

The head and rostellum (the round prominence on the scolex) of a tapeworm, which infects dogs and humans.

Photo by Carolina Biological Supply/Phototake

### TAPEWORMS

There are many species of tapeworm, all of which are carried by fleas! The most common tapeworm affecting dogs is known as *Dipylidium caninum*. The dog eats the flea and starts the tapeworm cycle. Humans can also be infected with tapeworms—so don't eat fleas! Fleas are so small that your dog could pass them onto your hands, your plate or your food and thus make it possible for you to ingest a flea that is carrying tapeworm eggs.

While tapeworm infection is not life-threatening in dogs (smart parasite!), it can be the cause of a very serious liver disease for humans. About 50% of the humans infected with *Echinococcus multilocularis*, a type of tapeworm that causes alveolar hydatid, perish.

### WHIPWORMS

In North America, whipworms are counted among the most common parasitic worms in dogs. The whipworm's scientific name is *Trichuris vulpis*. These worms attach themselves in the lower parts of the intestine, where they feed. Affected dogs may only experience upset tummies, colic and diarrhea. These worms, however, can live for months or years in the dog, beginning their larval stage in the small intestine, spending their adult stage in the large intestine and finally passing infective eggs through the dog's feces. The only way to detect whipworms is through a fecal examination, though this is not always foolproof. Treatment for whipworms is tricky, due to the worms' unusual life-cycle pattern, and very often dogs are reinfected due to exposure to infective eggs on the ground. The whipworm eggs can survive in the environment for as long as five years, thus cleaning up droppings in your own backyard as well as in public places is absolutely essential for sanitation purposes and the health of your dog and others.

### THREADWORMS

Though less common than roundworms, hookworms and those previously mentioned, threadworms concern dog owners in the Southwestern US and Gulf Coast area where the climate is hot and humid. Living in the small intestine of the dog, this worm measures a mere 2 millimeters and is round in shape. Like that of the whipworm, the threadworm's life cycle is very complex and the eggs and larvae are passed through the feces. A deadly disease in humans, *Strongyloides* readily infects people, and the handling of feces is the most common means of transmission. Threadworms are most often seen in young puppies; bloody diarrhea and pneumonia are symptoms. Sick puppies must be isolated and treated immediately; vets recommend a follow-up treatment one month later.

## HEARTWORM PREVENTATIVES

There are many heartworm preventatives on the market, many of which are sold at your veterinarian's office. These products can be given daily or monthly, depending on the manufacturer's instructions. All of these preventatives contain chemical insecticides directed at killing heartworms, which leads to some controversy among dog owners. In effect, heartworm preventatives are necessary evils, though you should determine how necessary based on your pet's lifestyle. There is no doubt that heartworm is a dreadful disease that threatens the lives of dogs. However, the likelihood of your dog's being bitten by an infected mosquito is slim in most places, and a mosquito-repellent (or an herbal remedy such as Wormwood or Black Walnut) is much safer for your dog and will not compromise his immune system (the way heartworm preventatives will). Should you decide to use the traditional preventative "medications," you can consider giving the pill every other or third month. Since the toxins in the pill will kill the heartworms at all stages of development, the pill would be effective in killing larvae, nymphs or adults and it takes four months for the larvae to reach the adult stage. Thus, there is no rationale to poisoning the dog's system on a monthly basis. Lastly, do not give the pill during the winter months since there are no mosquitoes around to pass on their infection, unless you live in a tropical environment.

## Life Cycle of the Heartworm

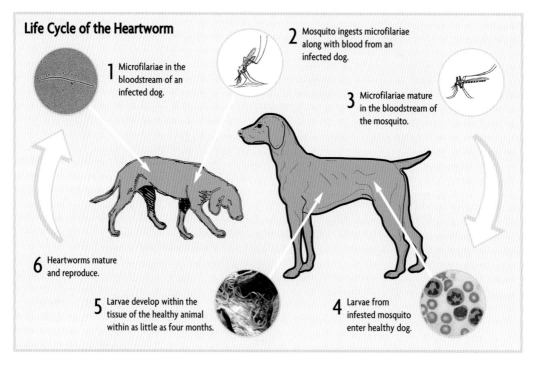

1 Microfilariae in the bloodstream of an infected dog.

2 Mosquito ingests microfilariae along with blood from an infected dog.

3 Microfilariae mature in the bloodstream of the mosquito.

4 Larvae from infested mosquito enter healthy dog.

5 Larvae develop within the tissue of the healthy animal within as little as four months.

6 Heartworms mature and reproduce.

### HEARTWORMS

Heartworms are thin, extended worms up to 12 inches long, which live in a dog's heart and the major blood vessels surrounding it. Dogs may have up to 200 worms. Symptoms may be loss of energy, loss of appetite, coughing, the development of a pot belly and anemia.

Heartworms are transmitted by mosquitoes. The mosquito drinks the blood of an infected dog and takes in larvae with the blood. The larvae, called microfilariae, develop within the body of the mosquito and are passed on to the next dog bitten after the larvae mature. It takes two to three weeks for the larvae to develop to the infective stage within the body of the mosquito. Dogs are usually treated at about six weeks of age and maintained on a prophylactic dose given monthly.

Blood testing for heartworms is not necessarily indicative of how seriously your dog is infected. Although this is a dangerous disease, it is not easy for a dog to be infected. Discuss the various preventatives with your vet, as there are many different types now available. Together you can decide on a safe course of prevention for your dog.

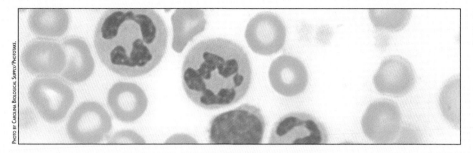

Magnified heart-worm larvae, *Diro-filaria immitis.*

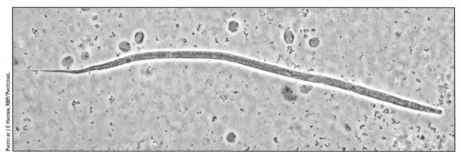

Heartworm, *Diro-filaria immitis.*

The heart of a dog infected with canine heart-worm, *Dirofilaria immitis.*

# HOMEOPATHY:
an alternative
to conventional
medicine

## "Less is Most"

Using this principle, the strength of a homeopathic remedy is measured by the number of serial dilutions that were undertaken to create it. The greater the number of serial dilutions, the greater the strength of the homeopathic remedy. The potency of a remedy that has been made by making a dilution of 1 part in 100 parts (or 1/100) is 1c or 1cH. If this remedy is subjected to a series of further dilutions, each one being 1/100, a more dilute and stronger remedy is produced. If the remedy is diluted in this way six times, it is called 6c or 6cH. A dilution of 6c is 1 part in 1,000,000,000,000. In general, higher potencies in more frequent doses are better for acute symptoms and lower potencies in more infrequent doses are more useful for chronic, long-standing problems.

## CURING OUR DOGS NATURALLY

Holistic medicine means treating the whole animal as a unique, perfect living being. Generally, holistic treatments do not suppress the symptoms that the body naturally produces, as do most medications prescribed by conventional doctors and vets. Holistic methods seek to cure disease by regaining balance and harmony in the patient's environment. Some of these methods include use of nutritional therapy, herbs, flower essences, aromatherapy, acupuncture, massage, chiropractic and, of course, the most popular holistic approach, homeopathy.

Homeopathy is a theory or system of treating illness with small doses of substances which, if administered in larger quantities, would produce the symptoms that the patient already has. This approach is often described as "like cures like." Although modern veterinary medicine is geared toward the "quick fix," homeopathy relies on the belief that, given the time, the body is able to heal itself and return to its natural, healthy state.

Choosing a remedy to cure a problem in our dogs is the difficult part of homeopathy. Consult with your vet for a professional diagnosis of your dog's symptoms. Often these symptoms require

immediate conventional care. If your vet is willing and knowledgeable, you may attempt a homeopathic remedy. Be aware that cortisone prevents homeopathic remedies from working. There are hundreds of possibilities and combinations to cure many problems in dogs, from basic physical problems such as excessive shedding, fleas or other parasites, unattractive doggy odor, bad breath, upset tummy, obesity, dry, oily or dull coat, diarrhea, ear problems or eye discharge (including tears and dry or mucousy matter), to behavioral abnormalities such as fear of loud noises, habitual licking, poor appetite, excessive barking and various phobias. From alumina to zincum metallicum, the remedies span the planet and the imagination...from flowers and weeds to chemicals, insect droppings, diesel smoke and volcanic ash.

## Using "Like to Treat Like"

Unlike conventional medicines that suppress symptoms, homeopathic remedies treat illnesses with small doses of substances that, if administered in larger quantities, would produce the symptoms that the patient already has. While the same homeopathic remedy can be used to treat different symptoms in different dogs, here are some interesting remedies and their uses.

### Apis Mellifica
(made from honey bee venom) can be used for allergies or to reduce swelling that occurs in acutely infected kidneys.

### Diesel Smoke
can be used to help control travel sickness.

### Calcarea Fluorica
(made from calcium fluoride, which helps harden bone structure) can be useful in treating hard lumps in tissues.

### Natrum Muriaticum
(made from common salt, sodium chloride) is useful in treating thin, thirsty dogs.

### Nitricum Acidum
(made from nitric acid) is used for symptoms you would expect to see from contact with acids, such as lesions, especially where the skin joins the linings of body orifices or openings such as the lips and nostrils.

### Symphytum
(made from the herb Knitbone, *Symphytum officinale*) is used to encourage bones to heal.

### Urtica Urens
(made from the common stinging nettle) is used in treating painful, irritating rashes.

## CDS: COGNITIVE DYSFUNCTION SYNDROME
### *"Old-Dog Syndrome"*

There are many ways for you to evaluate old-dog syndrome. Veterinarians have defined CDS (cognitive dysfunction syndrome) as the gradual deterioration of cognitive abilities. These are indicated by changes in the dog's behavior. When a dog changes his routine response, and maladies have been eliminated as the cause of these behavioral changes, then CDS is the usual diagnosis.

More than half the dogs over eight years old suffer some form of CDS. The older the dog, the more chance he has of suffering from CDS. In humans, doctors often dismiss the CDS behavioral changes as part of "winding down."

There are four major signs of CDS: frequent potty accidents inside the home, sleeping much more or much less than normal, acting confused and failing to respond to social stimuli.

### SYMPTOMS OF CDS

#### FREQUENT POTTY ACCIDENTS
- *Urinates in the house.*
- *Defecates in the house.*
- *Doesn't signal that he wants to go out.*

#### SLEEP PATTERNS
- *Moves much more slowly.*
- *Sleeps more than normal during the day.*
- *Sleeps less during the night.*

#### CONFUSION
- *Goes outside and just stands there.*
- *Appears confused with a faraway look in his eyes.*
- *Hides more often.*
- *Doesn't recognize friends.*
- *Doesn't come when called.*
- *Walks around listlessly and without a destination.*

#### FAILURE TO RESPOND TO SOCIAL STIMULI
- *Comes to people less frequently, whether called or not.*
- *Doesn't tolerate petting for more than a short time.*
- *Doesn't come to the door when you return home.*

The term *old* is a qualitative term. For dogs, as well as their masters, old is relative. Certainly we can all distinguish between a puppy Cocker Spaniel and an adult Cocker Spaniel—there are the obvious physical traits, such as size, appearance and facial expressions, and personality traits. Puppies and young dogs like to play with children. Children's natural exuberance is a good match for the seemingly endless energy of young dogs. They like to run, jump, chase and retrieve. When dogs grow up and cease their interaction with children, they are often thought of as being too old to play with the kids. On the other hand, if a Cocker Spaniel is only exposed to people with quieter lifestyles, his life will normally be less active and the decrease in his activity level as he ages will not be as obvious.

If people live to be 100 years old, dogs live to be 20 years old. This may sound like a good rule of thumb, but it is not particularly accurate. When trying to compare dog years to human years, you cannot make a generalization about all dogs. You can say that 12 to 13 years is a good lifespan for a Cocker Spaniel, which is a relatively good lifespan for any dog. You cannot make the same prediction for all breeds, as every breed develops differently. Very large breeds, for example, have shorter life expectancies than small breeds, and Toy breeds typically live the longest.

## WHAT TO LOOK FOR IN SENIORS

Most veterinarians and behaviorists use the seven-year mark as the time to consider a dog a *senior*.

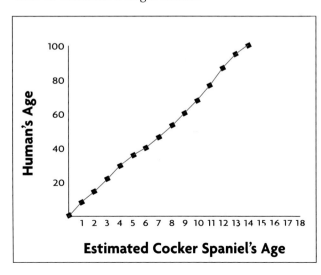

**Estimated Cocker Spaniel's Age**

This term does not imply that the dog is geriatric and has begun to fail in mind and body. Aging is essentially a slowing process. Humans readily admit that they feel a difference in their activity level from age 20 to 30, and then from 30 to 40, etc. By treating the seven-year-old dog as a senior, owners are able to implement certain therapeutic and preventive medical strategies with the help of their veterinarians.

A senior-care program should

### NOTICING THE SYMPTOMS

The symptoms listed below are symptoms that gradually appear and become more noticeable. They are not life-threatening; however, the symptoms below are to be taken very seriously and warrant a discussion with your veterinarian:

- Your dog cries and whimpers when he moves, and he stops running completely.
- Convulsions start or become more serious and frequent. The usual convulsion (spasm) is when the dog stiffens and starts to tremble, being unable or unwilling to move. The seizure usually lasts for 5 to 30 minutes.
- Your dog drinks more water and urinates more frequently. Wetting and bowel accidents take place indoors without warning.
- Vomiting becomes more and more frequent.

include at least two veterinary visits per year and screening sessions to determine the dog's health status, as well as nutritional counseling. Veterinarians determine the senior dog's health status through a blood smear for a complete blood count, serum chemistry profile with electrolytes, urinalysis, blood pressure check, electrocardiogram, ocular tonometry (pressure on the eyeball) and dental prophylaxis.

Such an extensive program for senior dogs is well advised before owners start to see the obvious physical signs of aging, such as slower and inhibited movement, graying, increased sleep/nap periods and disinterest in play and other activity. This preventative program promises a longer, healthier life for the aging dog. Among the physical problems common in aging dogs are the loss of sight and hearing, arthritis, kidney and liver failure, diabetes mellitus, heart disease and Cushing's disease (a hormonal disease).

In addition to the physical manifestations discussed, there are some behavioral changes and problems related to aging dogs. Dogs suffering from hearing or vision loss, dental discomfort or arthritis can become aggressive. Likewise, the near-deaf and/or blind dog may be startled more easily and react in an unexpectedly aggressive manner. Seniors suffering from senility can become

# WHEN YOUR DOG GETS OLD...
## SIGNS THE OWNER CAN LOOK FOR

| IF YOU NOTICE... | IT COULD INDICATE... |
| --- | --- |
| Discoloration of teeth and gums, foul breath, loss of appetite | Abcesses, gum disease, mouth lesions |
| Lumps, bumps, cysts, warts, fatty tumors | Cancers, benign or malignant |
| Cloudiness of eyes, apparent loss of sight | Cataracts, lenticular sclerosis, PRA, retinal dysplasia, blindness |
| Flaky coat, alopecia (hair loss) | Hormonal problems, hypothyroidism |
| Obesity, appetite loss, excessive weight gain | Various problems |
| Household accidents, increased urination | Diabetes, kidney or bladder disease |
| Increased thirst | Kidney disease, diabetes mellitus |
| Change in sleeping habits, coughing | Heart disease |
| Difficulty moving | Arthritis, degenerative joint disease, spondylosis (degenerative spine disease) |

**IF YOU NOTICE ANY OF THESE SIGNS, AN APPOINTMENT
SHOULD BE MADE IMMEDIATELY WITH A VETERINARIAN
FOR A THOROUGH EVALUATION.**

## DID YOU KNOW?
Your senior dog may lose interest in eating, not because he's less hungry but because his senses of smell and taste have diminished. The old chow simply does not smell as good as it once did. Additionally, older dogs use less energy and thereby can sustain themselves on less food.

The senior Cocker cannot perform the activities he did in his youth. His muzzle will become gray and he will sleep longer hours. Your old friend deserves special attention in his golden years.

more impatient and irritable. Housesoiling accidents are associated with loss of mobility, kidney problems and loss of sphincter control as well as plaque accumulation, physiological brain changes and reactions to medications. Older dogs, just like young puppies, can suffer from separation anxiety, which can lead to excessive barking, whining, housesoiling and destructive behavior. Seniors may become fearful of everyday sounds, such as vacuum cleaners, heaters, thunder and passing traffic. Some dogs have difficulty sleeping, due to discomfort, the need for frequent toilet visits and the like.

Owners should avoid spoiling the older dog with too many treats. Obesity is a common problem in older dogs and subtracts years from their lives. Keep the senior dog as trim as possible since excess weight puts additional stress on the body's vital organs. Some breeders recommend supplementing the diet with foods high in fiber and lower in calories. Adding fresh vegetables and marrow broth to the senior's diet makes a tasty, low-calorie, low-fat supplement. Vets also offer specialty diets for senior dogs that are worth exploring.

Your dog, as he nears his twilight years, needs his owner's patience and good care more than ever. Never punish an older dog for an accident or abnormal behavior. For all the years of love, protection and companionship that your dog has provided, he deserves special attention and courtesies. The older dog may

### CONSISTENCY COUNTS

Puppies and older dogs are very similar in their need for consistency in their lives. Older pets may experience hearing and vision loss, or may just be more easily confused by changes in their homes. Try to keep things consistent for the senior dog. For example, doors that are always open or closed should remain so. Most importantly, don't dismiss a pet just because he's getting old; most senior dogs remain active and important parts of their owners' lives.

need to relieve himself at 3 a.m. because he can no longer hold it for eight hours. Older dogs may not be able to remain crated for more than two or three hours. It may be time to give up a sofa or chair to your old friend. Although he may not seem as enthusiastic about your attention and petting, he does appreciate the considerations you offer as he gets older.

Your Cocker Spaniel does not understand why his world is slowing down. Owners must make their dogs' transition into the golden years as pleasant and rewarding as possible.

## WHAT TO DO WHEN THE TIME COMES

You are never fully prepared to make a rational decision about putting your dog to sleep. It is very obvious that you love your Cocker Spaniel or you would not be reading this book. Putting a loved dog to sleep is extremely difficult. It is a decision that must be made with your veterinarian. You are usually forced to make the decision when your Cocker experiences one or more life-threatening symptoms, causing you to seek veterinary help.

If the prognosis of the malady indicates that the end is near and your beloved pet will only suffer more and experience no enjoyment for the balance of his life, then euthanasia is the right choice.

### WHAT IS EUTHANASIA?

Euthanasia derives from the Greek, meaning *good death*. In other words, it means the planned, painless killing of a dog suffering from a painful, incurable condition, or who is so aged that he cannot walk, see, eat or control his excretory functions.

Euthanasia is performed by the vet, and is usually accomplished by injection with an overdose of an anesthesia or barbiturate. Aside from the prick of the needle, the experience is usually painless.

### MAKING THE DECISION

The decision to euthanize your dog is never easy. The days during which the dog becomes ill and the end occurs can be unusually stressful for you. If this is your

---

**HORMONAL PROBLEMS**
Although graying is normal and expected in older dogs, a flaky coat or loss of hair is not. Such coat problems may point to a hormonal problem. Hypothyroidism, in which the thyroid gland fails to produce the normal amount of hormones, is one such problem. Your veterinarian can treat hypothyroidism with an oral supplement. The condition is more common in certain breeds, so discuss its likelihood in your dog with your breeder and vet.

An older dog will especially appreciate a soft cozy bed in which he can make himself comfortable and warm.

first experience with the death of a loved one, you may need the comfort dictated by your religious beliefs. If you are the head of the family and have children, you should have involved them in the decision of putting your Cocker Spaniel to sleep. Usually your dog can be maintained on drugs in the vet's clinic for a few days in order to give you ample time to make a decision. During this time, talking with members of your family or even people who have lived through the same experience can ease the burden of your inevitable decision.

### THE FINAL RESTING PLACE

Dogs can have some of the same privileges as humans. They can be buried in pet cemeteries, which is generally expensive, or, if they have died at home, can be buried in your yard in a place suitably marked with a stone or a newly planted tree or bush. Alternatively, dogs can be cremated and the ashes returned to you, or some people prefer to leave their dogs at the vet's clinic.

All of these options should be discussed frankly and openly with your veterinarian. Do not be afraid to ask financial questions. Crema-

tions can be individual, but a less expensive option is mass cremation, although of course the ashes cannot then be returned. Vets can usually arrange cremation services on your behalf, or help you locate a pet cemetery if you choose one of these options.

### GETTING ANOTHER DOG?

The grief of losing your beloved dog will be as lasting as the grief of losing a human friend or relative. In most cases, if your dog died of old age (if there is such a thing), he had slowed down considerably. Do you want a new Cocker puppy to replace him? Or are you better off in finding a more mature Cocker Spaniel, say two to three years of age, which

will usually be house-trained and will have an already developed personality. In this case, you can find out if you like each other after a few hours of being together.

The decision is, of course, your own. Do you want another Cocker Spaniel or perhaps a different breed so as to avoid comparison with your beloved friend? Most people usually stay with the same breed because they know (and love) the characteristics of that breed. Then, too, they often know people who have the same breed and perhaps they are lucky enough that a breeder whom they know and respect expects a litter soon. What could be better?

Ask your vet to help you locate a pet cemetery in your area.

Dogs can be cremated. Their ashes can be displayed in a suitable cemetery facility, such as that shown here.

# SHOWING YOUR

# COCKER SPANIEL

When you purchase your Cocker Spaniel, you will make it clear to the breeder whether you want one just as a loveable companion and pet, or if you hope to be buying a Cocker Spaniel with show prospects. No reputable breeder will sell you a young puppy and tell you that it is *definitely* of show quality, for so much can go wrong during the early months of a puppy's development. If you plan to show, what you will hopefully have acquired is a puppy with "show potential."

The first concept that the canine novice learns when watching a dog show is that each dog first competes against members of his own breed. Once the judge has selected the best member of each breed (Best of Breed), provided that the show is judged on a Group system, that chosen dog will compete with other dogs in his group. Finally, the dogs chosen first in each group will compete for Best in Show.

The second concept that you must understand is that the dogs are not actually compared against one another. The judge compares each dog against his breed standard, the written description of the ideal specimen that is approved by the American Kennel Club (AKC). While some early breed standards were indeed based on specific dogs that were famous or popular, many dedicated enthusiasts say that a perfect specimen, as described in the standard, has never walked into a show ring, has never been bred and, to the woe of dog breeders around the globe, does not exist. Breeders attempt to get as close to this ideal as possible with every litter, but theoretically the "perfect" dog is so elusive that it is impossible. (And if the "perfect" dog were born, breeders and judges would never agree that it was indeed "perfect.")

## AKC GROUPS

For showing purposes, the American Kennel Club divides its recognized breeds into seven groups: Sporting Dogs, Hounds, Working Dogs, Terriers, Toys, Non-Sporting Dogs and Herding Dogs.

Showing your Cocker is a wonderful activity for owner and dog alike. Conformation shows bring new challenges and rewards for dog fanciers around the world.

If you are interested in exploring the world of dog showing, your best bet is to join your local breed club or the national parent club, which is the American Spaniel Club (ASC). These clubs often host both regional and national specialties, shows only for Cocker Spaniels, which can include conformation as well as obedience and field trials. Even if you have no intention of competing with your Cocker Spaniel, a specialty is like a festival for lovers of the breed who congregate to share their favorite topic: the Cocker Spaniel! Clubs also send out newsletters, and some organize training days and seminars in order that people may learn more about their chosen breed. To locate the breed club closest to you, contact the ASC or the American Kennel Club, which furnishes the rules and regulations for all of these events plus general dog registration and other basic requirements of dog ownership.

In the US, the American Kennel Club offers three kinds of conformation shows: an all-breed show (for all AKC-recognized breeds), a specialty show (for one breed only, usually sponsored by

## SHOW RING ETIQUETTE

Just like with anything else, there is a certain etiquette to the show ring that can only be learned through experience. Showing your dog can be quite intimidating to you as a novice when it seems as if everyone else knows what they are doing. You can familiarize yourself with ring procedure beforehand by taking a class to prepare you and your dog for conformation showing or by talking with an experienced handler. When you are in the ring, listen and pay attention to the judge and follow his/her directions. Remember, even the most skilled handlers had to start somewhere. Keep it up and you too will become a proficient handler before too long!

the parent club) and a Group show (for all breeds in the group).

For a dog to become an AKC champion of record, the dog must accumulate 15 points at the shows from at least three different judges, including two "majors." A "major" is defined as a three-, four- or five-point win, and the number of points per win is determined by the number of dogs entered in the show on that day. Depending on the breed, the number of points that are awarded varies. In a breed as popular as the Cocker Spaniel, more dogs are needed to rack up the points. At any dog show, only one dog and one bitch of each breed can win points.

Dog showing does not offer "co-ed" classes. Dogs and bitches never compete against each other in the classes. Non-champion dogs are called "class dogs" because they compete in one of five classes. Dogs are entered in a particular class depending on their age and previous show wins. To begin, there is the Puppy Class (for 6- to 9-month-olds and for 9- to 12-month-olds); this class is followed by the Novice Class (for dogs that have not won any first prizes except in the Puppy Class or three first prizes in the Novice Class and have not accumulated any points toward their champion title); the Bred-by Exhibitor Class (for dogs handled by their breeders or handled by one of the breeder's immediate family); the American-bred Class (for dogs bred in the US) and the Open Class (for any dog that is not a champion).

The judge at the show begins judging the Puppy Class, first dogs and then bitches, and proceeds through the classes. The judge places his winners first through fourth in each class. In the Winners Class, the first-place winners of each class compete with one another to determine Winners Dog and Winners Bitch. The judge also places a Reserve Winners Dog and Reserve

Winners Bitch, which could be awarded the points in the case of a disqualification. The Winners Dog and Winners Bitch are the two that are awarded the points for the breed, then compete with any champions of record entered in the show. The judge reviews the Winners Dog, Winners Bitch and all of the champions (often called "specials") to select his Best of Breed. The Best of Winners is selected between the Winners Dog and Winners Bitch. Were one of these two to be selected Best of Breed, he or she would automatically be named Best of Winners as well. Finally the judge selects his Best of Opposite Sex to the Best of Breed winner.

At a Group show or all-breed show, the Best of Breed winners from each breed then compete against one another for Group One through Group Four. The judge compares each Best of Breed to its breed standard, and the dog that most closely lives up to the ideal for his breed is selected as Group One. Finally, all seven group winners (from the Sporting Group, Toy Group, Hound Group, etc.) compete for Best in Show.

To find out about dog shows in your area, you can subscribe to the American Kennel Club's monthly magazine, the *American Kennel Gazette* and the accompanying *Events Calendar*. You can also look in your local newspaper for advertisements for dog shows in your area or go on the Internet to the AKC's website, www.akc.org.

If your Cocker Spaniel is six months of age or older and registered with the AKC, you can enter him in a dog show where the breed is offered classes. Provided that your Cocker Spaniel does not have a disqualifying fault, he can compete. Only unaltered dogs can be entered in a dog show, so if you have spayed or neutered your Cocker Spaniel, your dog cannot compete in conformation shows. The reason for this is simple. Dog shows are the main forum to prove which representatives of a breed are worthy of being bred. Only dogs that have achieved championships—the AKC "seal of

The desired gait of a Cocker Spaniel must be coordinated, smooth and effortless. The judge evaluates the movement of each dog entered in the class. Proper gait denotes correct structure.

The Cocker stands on a table for evaluation so that he is at a suitable height for the judge's examination of structure and coat. Cockers are the only dogs in the Sporting Group to be examined on the table because they are the smallest.

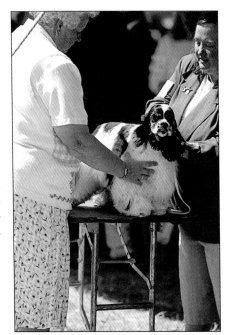

and from different angles, and approach the dog to check his teeth, overall structure, alertness and muscle tone, as well as consider how well the dog "conforms" to the standard. Most importantly, the judge will have the exhibitor move the dog around the ring in some pattern that he should specify (another advantage to not going first, but always listen since some judges change their directions—and the judge is always right!). Finally, the judge will give the dog one last look before moving on to the next exhibitor.

If you are not in the top four in your class at your first show,

approval" for quality in pure-bred dogs—should be bred. Altered dogs, however, can participate in other AKC events such as obedience trials and the Canine Good Citizen program.

Before you actually step into the ring, you would be well advised to sit back and observe the judge's ring procedure. If it is your first time in the ring, do not be over-anxious and run to the front of the line. It is much better to stand back and study how the exhibitor in front of you is performing. The judge asks each handler to "stack" the dog, hope-fully showing the dog off to his best advantage. The judge will observe the dog from a distance

**CLUB CONTACTS**

You can get information about dog shows from the national kennel clubs:

American Kennel Club
5580 Centerview Dr.
Raleigh, NC 27606-3390
www.akc.org

United Kennel Club
100 E. Kilgore Road
Kalamazoo, MI 49002
www.ukcdogs.com

Canadian Kennel Club
89 Skyway Ave., Suite 100, Etobicoke, Ontario
M9W 6R4 Canada
www.ckc.ca

The Kennel Club
1-5 Clarges St., Piccadilly, London
W1Y 8AB, UK
www.the-kennel-club.org.uk

do not be discouraged. Be patient and consistent, and you may eventually find yourself in a winning line-up. Remember that the winners were once in your shoes and have devoted many hours and much money to earn the placement. If you find that your dog is losing every time and never getting a nod, it may be time to consider a different dog sport or to just enjoy your Cocker Spaniel as a pet. Parent clubs offer other events, such as agility, tracking, obedience, field events and more, which may be of interest to the owner of a well-trained Cocker Spaniel.

## OBEDIENCE TRIALS

Obedience trials in the US trace back to the early 1930s, when organized obedience training was developed to demonstrate how well dog and owner could work together. The pioneer of obedience trials is Mrs. Helen Whitehouse Walker, a Standard Poodle

The Cocker's field and hunting instincts have been channeled toward many other arenas. The goal-motivated Cocker is very enthusiastic about training for and participating in agility trials. This is Alex, owned by Jim Larsen.

The Westminster
Kennel Club Dog
Show is America's
most prestigious
show and the oldest
dog show in the
world. Cocker
Spaniels took Best in
Show honors on four
occasions in the 20th
century.

fancier, who designed a series of exercises after the Associated Sheep, Police Army Dog Society of Great Britain. Since the days of Mrs. Walker, obedience trials have grown by leaps and bounds, and today there are over 2,000 trials held in the US every year, with more than 100,000 dogs competing. Any registered AKC dog can enter an obedience trial, regardless of conformational disqualifications or neutering.

Obedience trials are divided into three levels of progressive difficulty. At the first level, the Novice, dogs compete for the title Companion Dog (CD); at the intermediate level, the Open, dogs compete for the title Companion Dog Excellent (CDX); and at the advanced level, the Utility, dogs compete for the title Utility Dog (UD). Classes are sub-divided into "A" (for beginners) and "B" (for more experienced handlers). A perfect score at any level is 200, and a dog must score 170 or better to earn a "leg," of which three are needed to earn the title. To earn points, the dog must score more than 50% of the available points in each exercise; the possible points range from 20 to 40.

Each level consists of a differ-ent set of exercises. In the Novice level, the dog must heel on- and off-leash, come, long sit, long down and stand for examination. These skills are the basic ones

**SHOW-QUALITY SHOWS**
While you may purchase a puppy in the hope of having a successful career in the show ring, it is impossi-ble to tell, at eight to ten weeks of age, whether your dog will be a contender. Some promising pups end up with minor to serious faults that prevent them from taking home an award, but this certainly does not mean they can't be the best of companions for you and your family. To find out if your potential show dog is show-quality, enter him in a match to see how a judge evaluates him. You may also take him back to your breeder as he matures to see what he might advise.

required for a well-behaved "Companion Dog." The Open level requires that the dog perform the exercises previously mentioned but without a leash for extended lengths of time, as well as retrieve a dumbbell, broad jump and drop on recall. In the Utility level, dogs must perform ten difficult exercises, including scent discrimination, hand signals for basic commands, directed jump and directed retrieve.

Once a dog has earned the UD title, he can compete with other proven obedience dogs for the coveted title of Utility Dog Excellent (UDX), which requires that the dog win "legs" in ten shows. Utility Dogs who earn "legs" in Open B and Utility B earn points toward their Obedience Trial Champion title. In 1977, the title Obedience Trial Champion (OTCh.) was established by the AKC. To become an OTCh., a dog needs to earn 100 points, which requires three first places in Open B and Utility under three different judges.

The Grand Prix of obedience trials, the AKC National Obedience Invitational gives qualifying Utility Dogs the chance to win the newest and highest title: National Obedience Champion (NOC). Only the top 25 ranked obedience dogs, plus any dog ranked in the top 3 in its breed, are allowed to compete.

## AGILITY TRIALS

Having had its origins in the UK back in 1977, AKC agility had its official beginning in the US in August 1994, when the first licensed agility trials were held. The AKC allows all registered breeds (including Miscellaneous Class breeds) to participate, providing the dog is 12 months of age or older. Agility is designed so that the handler demonstrates how well the dog can work at his side. The handler directs his dog over an obstacle course that includes jumps as well as tires, the dog walk, weave poles, pipe tunnels, collapsed tunnels, etc. While working his way through the course, the dog must keep one eye and ear on the

This obstacle is called the dog walk and requires great balance for the participating Cocker. Fortunately, Cockers move with coordination and grace, and can usually handle this obstacle with proper instruction and assistance.

After maneuvering through the weave poles, this Cocker eagerly awaits his next task.

## CANINE GOOD CITIZEN®

Have you ever considered getting your dog "certified"? The AKC's Canine Good Citizen® Program affords your dog just that opportunity. Your dog shows that he is a well-behaved canine citizen, using the basic training and good manners you have taught him, by taking a series of ten tests that illustrate that he can behave properly at home, in a public place and around other dogs. The tests are administered by participating dog clubs, colleges, 4-H clubs, scouts and other community groups and are open to all pure-bred and mixed-breed dogs. Upon passing the ten tests, the suffix CGC is then applied to your dog's name.

The ten tests are: 1. Accepting a friendly stranger; 2. Sitting politely for petting; 3. Appearance and grooming; 4. Walking on a lead; 5. Walking through a group of people; 6. Sit, down and stay on command; 7. Coming when called; 8. Meeting another dog; 9. Calm reaction to distractions; 10. Separation from owner.

handler and the rest of his body on the course. The handler gives verbal and hand signals to guide the dog through the course.

The first organization to promote agility trials in the US was the United States Dog Agility Association, Inc. (USDAA), which was established in 1986 and spawned numerous member clubs around the country. Both the USDAA and the AKC offer titles to winning dogs. Three titles are available through the USDAA: Agility Dog (AD), Advanced Agility Dog (AAD) and Master Agility Dog (MAD). The AKC offers Novice Agility (NA), Open Agility (OA), Agility Excellent (AX) and Master Agility Excellent (MX). Beyond these four AKC titles, dogs can win additional ones in "jumper" classes, Jumpers with Weave Novice (NAJ), Open (OAJ) and Excellent (MXJ), which lead to the ultimate title(s): MACH, Master Agility Champion. Dogs

This Cocker Spaniel is methodically handling the A-frame at an agility trial. He works with speed, balance and determination.

can continue to add number designations to the MACH titles, indicating how many times the dog has met the MACH requirements, such as MACH1, MACH2, and so on.

Agility is great fun for dog and owner with many rewards for everyone involved. Interested owners should join a training club that has obstacles and experienced agility handlers who can introduce owner and dog to the "ropes" (and tires, tunnels, etc.).

### TRACKING

Any dog is capable of tracking, using his nose to follow a trail, and the Cocker has quite a nose! Tracking tests are exciting and competitive ways to test your

What a feeling of pride to have a successful day in the show ring!

Cocker Spaniel's scenting ability. The AKC started tracking tests in 1937, when the first AKC-licensed test took place as part of the Utility level at an obedience trial. Ten years later in 1947, the AKC offered the first title, Tracking Dog (TD). It was not until 1980 that the AKC added the title Tracking Dog Excellent (TDX), which was followed by the title Versatile Surface Tracking (VST) in 1995. The title Champion Tracker (CT) is awarded to a dog who has earned all three titles.

In the beginning level of tracking, the owner follows the dog through a field on a long leash. To earn the TD title, the dog must follow a track laid by a human 30 to 120 minutes prior. The track is about 500 yards long with up to 5 directional changes. The TDX requires that the dog follow a track that is 3 to 5 hours old over a course up to 1,000 yards long with up to 7 directional changes. The VST requires that the dog follow a track up to 5 hours old through an urban setting.

### FIELD TRIALS

Field trials are offered to the retrievers, pointers and spaniel breeds of the Sporting Group as well as to the Beagles, Dachshunds and Bassets of the Hound Group. The purpose of field trials is to demonstrate a dog's ability to perform his breed's original purpose in the field. The events vary depending on the type of dog but, in all trials, dogs compete against one another for placement and for points toward their Field Champion (FC) titles.

The Cocker Spaniel competes in field trials designed for flushing dogs; the other breeds included in this category are the English Cocker Spaniel, Clumber Spaniel, English Springer Spaniel, Field Spaniel, Sussex Spaniel and Welsh Springer Spaniel. The dogs are to search and locate game birds within the hunter's range, flush the birds into the air and then retrieve the downed game on command.

The AKC offers the very prestigious Dual Champion title for dogs that attain their FC title as well as their Champion title in conformation. Dogs that earn this dual title prove that they have the beauty required for the show ring but have not lost the original and intended characteristics of their breed. There are many Cocker Dual Champions, thus proving wrong those that think the heavily coated breed is incapable of a day's work. There are other organizations in the US that organize their own field trials and offer their own titles, separate from those of the AKC.

**HUNTING TESTS**
The AKC instituted its hunting tests in June 1985 and their

Although the smallest of the sporting spaniels, the Cocker cannot be deterred from succeeding in many areas of competition.

popularity has grown tremendously. The AKC offers three titles at hunting tests: Junior Hunter (JH), Senior Hunter (SH) and Master Hunter (MH). Each title requires that the dog earn qualifying "legs" at the tests: the JH requiring four; the SH, five; and the MH, six.

Hunting tests are not competitive like field trials, and participating dogs are judged against a standard set forth by the AKC. Each dog's hunting abilities are evaluated, and there is no limit to how many dogs can qualify as long as they earn the necessary points.

Due to their natural instincts and skills, Cocker Spaniels can be very successful in hunting tests. The first Cocker to earn the prestigious Master Hunter title was Ch. Pett's Southwest Breeze.

# My Cocker Spaniel

PUT YOUR PUPPY'S FIRST PICTURE HERE

Dog's Name _____

Date _____ Photographer _____